Let's Write A Story

CREATING A GREAT VILLAIN

Sue Viders and Becky Martinez

DENVER, CO

Copyright © 2019 Viders and Martinez
Let's Write a Story…Creating a Great Villain
ISBN - 978-0-942011-36-4

Contents

1 -- Our Love Affair with Villains

2 -- The World of Villains

3 -- The Importance of Villains

4 -- Creating Your Villain

5 -- The Role of Your Villain

6 -- The Hero-Villain Relationship

7 -- The Villain's Arc

8 -- The Villain's Resolution

9 -- Minor Villains

10 – Summary

Getting Started

There is one great truth in writing great fiction, and it is...

All great stories have a great villain!

If there is no villain, there is no story.
>No one for the hero/heroine to oppose
>No one to cause conflict
>No one to finally defeat.

Think of the stories you have read, and recall those that stay with you.
>What are they?
>Why do you remember them?

Right!

>>You remember the villains.
>>You recall the problems they caused – big and little.
>>You remember how the main characters fought back

SUE VIDERS AND BECKY MARTINEZ

You were gripped by the thrilling battles, but...
You were pleased at how the heroes/heroines won

In some stories the characters you loved/hated and remembered the most was...right...the villain.

The following pages are full of ideas and suggestions for you to ponder and use in the novel you are writing.

Enjoy reminders of familiar villains as you learn how to create your own story villains. But, please, after checking them all out, let us know your thoughts. We would appreciate your feedback on villains of all ages, shapes and genres.

sueviders@comcast.net
beckmartinez77@aol.com

CHAPTER 1

Our Love Affair with Villains

*Each film (story) is only as good as its villain.
Since the heroes and gimmicks tend to repeat from film to film,
only a great villain can transform a good try into a
triumph.*
Robert Ebert film critic

Villains are all around us in real life, and while we may not want to deal with them in our world, as readers, we thrill to their antics and tricks in books, movies and plays. They provide the challenges that can bring out the best in our favorite fictional characters. As long as storytellers have been weaving tales of great triumph or sorrow, listeners, readers, and viewers have loved to hate great villains.

Our main characters in fiction can be ordinary people enduring or facing superhuman challenges. We may want them to be like us, but to be us when we are at our best. We actually prefer them to be even better. We want them to be stronger versions, who may be challenged, but we want them to prevail in the end and achieve a happy ending to their story.

On the other hand, we want them to tackle villains of all sizes and shapes who manage to make their lives and the lives of others around them miserable. Villains may appear in human form, disguised as best friends, or they might be the angry competitor out to win at all costs or the madman aiming for world domination. They might be the beautiful woman who seeks to use her looks to get ahead or the pitiful creature who evokes sympathy only to later turn into a murderous monster.

Real life villains can be as simple as the nasty or negative people around us on a personal basis, or they can be found as we watch daily newscasts and witness enemies trying to outsmart their foes using nefarious methods. We can witness or read stories of politicians ignoring ethics rules or bankers embezzling from their clients or family squabbles that end up in murder.

Writers can get ideas for the villains they create from many sources—from the daily news stories to the nasty person next door to an idea that springs from their own imagination. In this book, we will focus on creating fictional villains of all shapes and sizes. These villains are not confined to human forms. They can also be animals, creatures of any ilk or some sort of robotic entity. They can come from outer space or the deepest recesses of the Earth. They also don't need to be any living creature at all. They might also show up in a natural form as giant threatening storms or icebergs that appear benign on the surface. They might also be mythical creatures of all shapes and sizes. They can be as large as a planet or as small as a microscopic element. They can be as hugely devastating as a giant superstorm, earthquake, erupting volcano or as small as a flea or the virus infecting the flea. Villains can come from anywhere. As Hollywood has shown us, villains can even appear as fictional storms mixed with animals, like a *Sharknado*.

As evidenced by that last example, the world of villains is limited only by a writer's imagination. The purpose of this book is to introduce writers to villains of all types, sizes, and dimensions, and then show how to make the best use of those antagonists in stories, books, movies, and plays. Throughout this book, we will present definitions, motives, and descriptions of some of the best-known villains from the world of the arts, literature, movies, and television. We'll also go back to legends, fairy tales, folklore, mythology, and religious stories to illustrate how long villains have played a role in various societies.

We begin with the premise that there is one thing a great villain must do in any work of fiction. Whether truly evil, threatening world domination or global destruction, or simply someone whose goals and wants are different from the hero or heroine, the villain should cause *conflict* and be a *driving force* in the story. The villain can be a super villain with frightening superpowers, or it could be a creature of epic proportions or as ethereal as a strange belief hidden in an ordinary person's mind. The villain can be challenging physically, like a superstorm, or it can be an internal mental threat poised to destroy the hero or heroine's normal world. It can also be a romantic rival out to win the heart of the hero or heroine.

No matter its shape, form, or origin, the villain of a story has to be acceptable to the readers/viewers—even if not totally believable--so readers can root for his/her/its demise or for the hero/heroine to overcome whatever problem that the villain represents. Some villains may challenge credulity in their form or shape, but as long as the readers or viewers accept the concept of their evil-doing, any villain can work in a story.

While the villain can challenge the lives of everyone in a story, for the true villain to work—they or it—should pose a danger to the hero, heroine, or the people the good folks love. The villain doesn't need to see the struggle as personal, but the story will be stronger if the hero or heroine views the confrontation that way. *Their* lives are in danger, or the lives of *their family* are threatened. The personal peril brings more emotion to the battle, and that direct challenge is what we love most about dealing with villains.

When villains threaten our heroes, we can see those bad guys as threats to ourselves as well. We want them to be taken seriously and then stopped or taken down, imprisoned, destroyed, or killed. However, the outcome is accomplished, we want the story concluded—even if it is only the current problem that is solved, and there could still be storm clouds in the distance. At this story's ending, we want the villains to be stopped or get "theirs" if they are not dead or wounded. They could spin off into space like Darth Vader, but they need to NOT achieve their goal.

We want the problem of the virus solved or the storm or the catastrophe dissipated by the end. There might be some major cleaning up to do, but the danger should be gone or leaving or vanquished for the moment. The heroes should have survived or overcome the villains' challenge or lessened the danger in the end. Our heroes can fear villains coming back, but this time around, those disastrous entities or evil people have been destroyed or decimated. The world is safe--at least for now.

That caveat is provided because just as readers love certain heroes, they also enjoy, admire or love to hate certain villains. Accordingly, writers should not underestimate the longevity of the villains they create. Many of the most popular villains regularly return to enact more evil deeds. We see them reappear in book and movie sequels or in comics, and on television.

Viewers and readers appear to never tire of watching dastardly, masterfully-written villains perform their wicked schemes. Who doesn't love to curl up late in the evening and watch Dracula threaten another town or go to a new James Bond film where the famous British spy is forced to out-think a bad guy such as Goldfinger, Biofeld or Scaramanga? Those classic villains from the past continue to enthrall new generations of readers and moviegoers.

For the writer who chooses to create a series, the great villain can return, just as a recurring hero or heroine might. The bad guy doesn't have to be limited to one story any more than the hero is. Great villains can appear in more than one book or movie. Voldemort, from the *Harry Potter* series, kept reappearing, as did Batman's Joker or Luke Skywalker's father, Darth Vader. They were villains who couldn't be vanquished in one story. They kept coming back and causing more trouble for our heroes and heroines. Because they were so powerful, readers and moviegoers enjoyed seeing them go head to head in different confrontations and different circumstances.

Smart villains like Moriarty, the man who so often fought Sherlock Holmes, also continue to be nasty role models for new creations by fledgling authors and aspiring screenwriters. Authors not only develop new villains, but they may also branch out to unleash new villains in a wide variety of genres, following the example of the creator of Moriarty, Sir Arthur Conan Doyle. He is still frightening readers with his nonhuman villains in the *Hound of the Baskervilles*. Current writers might also start in one medium or one genre and then branch out to create new villains for books or movies in different genres.

If you are an avid reader or moviegoer, you have come to know so many different types of villains in literature and movies, ranging from the intrepid Javert from *Les Misérables* to Dracula, to the spooky Mrs. Danvers in *Rebecca*, or more recently, Panem in *The Hunger Games*. Some villains border on the ridiculous such as the Big Bad Wolf in the *Three Little Pigs* while others, such as Hannibal (the

Cannibal) Lecter from *Silence of the Lambs*, are too scary to contemplate ever meeting in the real world.

Villains come in all sizes, shapes and blood colors, and vary from human beings, to Mother Nature to any number of aliens. In a romance,, the villain might be as scheming as a woman out to take away the heroine's beloved, such as Lucy Steele attempted to do to Elinor Dashwood in *Sense and Sensibility*. Computers, such as Hal in *2001* or man-eating, thinking plants like Audrey II, the blood-sucking plant in *Little Shop of Horrors,* can nearly bring a hero to his/her knees.

There are also the great animals that can challenge a person in a book or movie—from Herman Melville's great white whale in *Moby Dick* to the oversized man-eating shark in *Jaws*. Of course, there are also the great comic book villains like Loki or Lex Luthor from *Superman*. One of our favorite villains is Scar from *The Lion King* where the lion is fashioned after Claudius from Shakespeare's *Hamlet*.

Most villains are simply sad, unbalanced human beings, but their actions can range from simple bullying to spreading terror or a virus that could destroy the world. They might also be the creation of man or an experiment gone awry, such as the dinosaurs of Michael Crichton's *Jurassic Park* books and movies. The villains might be normal humans by day and turn to vampires or werewolves at night, or they could be shapeshifters who can change at a moment's notice due to a curse or a special potion.

While there may be no limits to how villains are created or who they are or what they become or how evil they might be, there are some general guidelines to keep in mind as you set out to formulate your plans for a story featuring unique villains.

Your villain will, to a great extent, depend on the genre, the type of plot or the theme of your story. Therefore, it helps to have at least a vague idea of who or what your villain is going to be when you start to write the story. For instance, is the real villain the mechanical creature? Or is the villain actually the human manipulating the dangerous creature? In *Jurassic Park II*, the human who had taken the mother T-Rex and her baby off the island was the real culprit. When they were returned to their island, they were no longer a threat.

If you are writing a science fiction story or fantasy, your villain might be an alien or creature of some sort. It could also be a foreign world or an unknown entity or space creature. You might also have a natural phenomenon, like a tornado, earthquake or tidal wave, as the source of the problem for the human hero or heroine.

The villain might be both human and natural, such as the case in the movie, *Titanic*. The iceberg was the catalyst, but the icy ocean was also a villain, threatening death as the ship sank. But there were human villains as well, with Rose's crazed fiancée trying to keep her while his valet tried to kill, the hero, Jack.

As you begin creating villains for your story, there are also other steps you can take in advance to make certain that the bad guys you create are memorable. You want YOUR villains to not only be more realistic and believable to your readers or audience but you also need to make them strong and unique.

Get to know other villains. Study fictional villains as you read novels or watch television programs or movies. Which villains appealed to you? Which ones do you remember the most? What made you remember them? Was it their actions that were memorable, or was it their underhanded methods that drew your interest? Perhaps it was the vicious way they perpetrated their crimes. What was it about them *personally* that might have appealed to you, even if they repelled you overall? Was it their extravagant lifestyle, their flashy clothes, their philosophy of life? Their intellectual speech? Did you understand them, admire their skills and still hate them?

Villains should appear unbeatable at the beginning. If you have a weak villain, then the person, entity, animal or creature could be defeated easily in the opening pages. You need to begin with such a strong villain that the hero/heroine doesn't know what to do to defeat this enemy. Challenge your heroes and heroines in a major way right from the start of your story.

Villains need a past. Like your heroes and heroines, villains should have a background story of their own, such as an event or person that turned them evil or made them corrupt. Perhaps the villain was born mean, but years of getting away with vile behavior might have solidified his/her evil personality. Villains might have been mistreated or cheated as a child and vowed to never let anyone get the best of them again. A villain might be a legend from the past or a theory of a possible event. The antagonist could also be something like a superstorm that has never been seen, but has often been predicted. Then it suddenly appears.

A human or legendary villain may have a sad background story, one with a tragic result that helped turn him/her/it turn "bad" or into the villain. For instance, perhaps ancestors from a certain village led the charge that destroyed the wolf pack or turned humans they hated into werewolves. Perhaps their descendants have now returned to wreak vengeance on the town and its current residents. The limits of a villain can stretch as far as the writer's imagination.

Villains can be the product of circumstance. For instance, a giant shark could be a villain, but the reason might be a matter of coincidence. In search of a new feeding area, it has settled near a populated coastal village. In the case of a giant tornado or iceberg, the problem could be the season or the area that spawns them. On the other hand, if you are dealing with people or animals, there should be a reason why the villains are in a position to wreak havoc. The problem could be as simple as being in the wrong place at the wrong time, such as the victims in *Titanic* or the visitors at *Jurassic Park III*, or it could be that the villain has followed the hero or still inhabits the area, like Stephen King's creature in his book, *It*.

Villains need flaws or weaknesses as well as strengths. Think about the possible flaws or weaknesses you could give to your villains. There should be a reason the villain is a bad or cruel person. While you want your villain to be strong in battling the hero, you also don't want to make the villain totally invincible. Real villains have weaknesses, just as heroes do, and you need to be able to use them in the story. A villain who is multi-dimensional is not only a stronger foe but is also more realistic and more believable.

Don't shortchange the reader or the villain. Look for ways to make your villains unique. Don't let the character become a simple cardboard cut-out or an ordinary bad guy. Make your villains unique to their particular circumstances and story just as your heroes and heroines are. Now that we have established some of those guidelines, you might be asking, how can *you* come up with good villains? How can *you* develop these unique characters? What about villains in your own life? Think about those people you might have come to consider as enemies. Why did that happen? Was it something personal or was there something in their character that turned you against them? Study stories about real people you might have heard about on the news who have done evil or corrupt things – like murder, betrayal or embezzling. What were their motives or what might have made them act in such a negative way? Make a list of negative characteristics from people you've either known or read about. You might even consider bad or irritating traits from your friends, family and acquaintances to create bad traits for your villains. As you contemplate creating a villain, ponder the good as well as the bad. What were "good" traits in the villains you remember or admire? Even great villains might have soft spots or things that they occasionally do that are not so bad, even if it is simply loving their dog or cat.

This book will explore the different sides of what makes up a good villain. We'll look at why villains are necessary for fictional stories, how to create the right villain for your story, and how to make the villain come alive for the reader. We'll also examine the role of lesser villains and their relationships to the hero and/or heroine as well as to the main villain.

Finally, we will guide you on how to put everything together to create a story that will challenge the heroes and heroines, make them grow and bring about a satisfying conclusion. The goal is to help you develop a story that leaves the reader wanting to read more books or short stories featuring your brand of villains. We have also taken the extra step of listing some of our favorite, memorable villains. These lists will be found at the end of every chapter. Nearly every reader or writer has their own personal list of their favorite nasty bad guys and gals. We have grouped our lists at the end of the chapters as the best "bad" examples of the various types of villains being discussed in each chapter. As you read through the various lists, you will undoubtedly find examples of your own to add.

Our Favorite Villains

Dracula — *Dracula* series
Darth Vader — *Star Wars* saga
Lord Voldemort - *Harry Potter* series
Moriarty — Sh*erlock Holmes* series
Hannibal Lecter — *Silence of the Lamb*

CHAPTER 2

The World of Villains

*As there is a use in medicine for poisons,
so, the world cannot move forward without rogues.*
Ralph Waldo Emerson

The great early American poet and philosophizer Ralph Waldo Emerson had exactly the right idea when he made that statement several centuries ago. Without rogues or villains of any kind, even when they are simply "beliefs," where would we get the conflict in a fictional story? There would be no turmoil, no disagreements, no problems--just a bunch of written or reported happenings and essays.

A great story, no matter what genre, no matter what media is used, needs the hero or heroine to be tested to make the story work. We need our heroes and heroines to exhibit their powers as they continue to grow and develop over the course of a story. They need to be able to question their own motives and perhaps grow and change their outlook on life as they face new foes and new circumstances. Heroes cannot prove themselves as the good guys if they have nothing to conquer, or there are no challenges to overcome or bad guys to vanquish in a story. Whether that fictional opponent is a super villain from another world, a disease or a creature that suddenly appears or is discovered, or a silly belief from the next-door neighbor who is determined to do things his/her way, the villain is as necessary to a story as any great hero or heroine. The Good cannot exist without the Bad.

If the hero or heroine is battling a storm or super virus, he and/or she must find a way around the antagonist (entity, storm) or a means to survive. Mainly, though, the villain or villainess is the character in your story who tries to keep the main character (no matter who or what this is) from achieving his, her or its goals, whether they are immediate goals like falling in love, getting through a snowstorm or long-term goals, like bringing a dying town back to life or conquering a planet threatened by alien forces.

Since the main objective of a villain is to cause CONFLICT in a story, most of the time this will be a person or thing, or things. However, in some genres, such as romance, the actual "villain" may not be a person. It may be a belief or powerful attitude that causes the CONFLICT between the main characters and keeps them apart. For instance, the villain could be the pagan law that requires young people to marry whomever the elders select or the society that requires a woman to marry the brother if her husband dies.

The dictionary says that a true villain is:

> A deliberate scoundrel or criminal
> A person or thing blamed for a particular evil
> A depraved, wicked, or vile character
> Someone capable or guilty of great crimes
> Evil or malevolent in nature

As we've already mentioned, throughout this book we will keep bringing in as many of our favorite movie, television and literary villains as we can. Different villains match different topics and while you may spot some repetition, we've tried to keep it to a minimum to get in as many variations as possible. The same is true with the real-life villains who have brought pain and woe to those around them. We also want to cover as many different types of villains as possible so some may fall into several categories. We also want to relate to many different types of readers and writers in a variety of genres. Hopefully, you may encounter some new villains to study as you make new discoveries.

Some common traits are shared by many villains. Nearly all the villainous characters we present may see themselves as powerful, superior to others and much more intelligent than the people around them or the population at large. They believe in living by their own personal code of rules, which they believe is the *only* way they can live. They may also create a code of their own, or select the rules for other villains.

They are also ruthless and determined to win at whatever they attempt at any cost and in any manner that allows them to emerge on top. They may protect some of those around them, or those who follow them, but in the end, they feel only *they* and *their* whims are what is important.

While these villains are strong and ruthless, not all fictional antagonists are out to rule the world. Some thrive on a small scale. Serial killer Norman Bates from the movie, *Psycho,* didn't leave the small California town where he lived when his mother died. Instead he remained in her house and turned the family motel into a death trap for young women passing through. Annie Wilkes in *Misery* didn't care to leave her country abode. She was happy to sit at home reading the books of her favorite author. She didn't turn into a crazed villain until she met that author and discovered he planned to bring an end to the character she had come to love.

Many villains can also be simply low-level bullies or angry people who have been thwarted by time or circumstances.
Consider the villain who is a father who wants the best for his daughter. He is totally opposed to her marrying the ordinary boy next door. Perhaps he doesn't want her marry to that boy because the kid always appeared to be a hopeless "loser" going nowhere in life because he sits around playing video games all day, he didn't graduate at the top of his class or play on the football team. The father would prefer his daughter date the well-dressed polite boys who are the sons of his business partners or a connected classmate bound for an Ivy League college or even a young business associate who shows more initiative.

In this type of romantic tale, the "villain" may actually be the father's *belief* or *attitude*, which needs to be changed or modified. Here the villain is WITHIN a character's own personality. The father loves his daughter—he simply wants to control her future. Usually this leads to the character (the father) being redeemed or outgrowing the negative, obsessive belief.

These types of villainous characters may be called *antagonists* because while they cause conflict in the story, they are not the evil sort of villains who cause death and destruction to those around them. They are lesser villains or opposing forces.

For instance, that father who didn't want his daughter to marry the "loser" next door might throw roadblocks in their way over the course of the story, but he isn't necessarily a physical danger to her or the boy. His antagonistic beliefs are the actual problem or the villain. In this sort of sweet romance, the plot might not include a dangerous struggle between the antagonist and the hero, but there will still be an ongoing battle.

The resolution may come when the boy makes a sacrifice that shows the father the depth of his feelings or the father realizes the boy has other attributes that suit his daughter better. Perhaps the daughter makes the sad decision to totally break free of her father's possessive grip and move away with the boy. If the man fears he might lose the daughter he loves forever, the final solution rests in his hands. He must make a choice—either find a way to accept the boy or lose his relationship with his precious daughter. In this case, the villain is beliefs, and each person must overcome or change them or discover what is most important in their lives to achieve the happy ending.

Let's continue to examine the roles of villains at different levels that you might want to use in your stories, novels, or screenplays:

The **Classic Villain** might include sociopaths or psychopaths, such as mentally unstable or revenge-seeking villains. These bad guys can be killers who don't care who they have to destroy to get their own way. A good example might be the Wicked Witch of the West from *The Wizard of Oz*. She was determined to get revenge for her sister's death, but she had also been terrorizing the people of Oz for years.

The **Supernatural Villain** might come from another realm, outer space or another time. This villain may possess unearthly powers that can't be explained. An example would be Lord Voldemort from the *Harry Potter* series with his magical powers or Darth Vader who uses his supernatural strength to keep planets under the control of the Empire.

While these types of villains may possess unusual or overwhelming power, they may also have some sort of weakness or Achilles "heel" that the hero can use to save the day. For instance, in the end, Darth Vader's feelings for his son, Luke, led to his downfall.

The alien creatures who came to Earth in the popular movie, *Signs,* seemed invincible at first as they took over cities and villages. However, it turned out they could not tolerate water. Once this weakness was revealed, they began leaving earth to go in search for a new planet where they could survive. In H. G. Wells' science fiction tale, *War of the Worlds,* alien creatures also appeared unstoppable, but they fell victim to the smallest weapons on earth—its bacteria and viruses.

Readers often enjoy **Redeemable Villains** who might have a change of heart and decide to mend their ways. Consider the case of Professor Snape in the Harry Potter series who was secretly in love with Harry's mother. Because of his feelings, he often watched out for the boy, even though he came off as the villain at times.

No matter which area you choose as a background for creating your villain, it is worth the time and effort to research the backstories of your favorite villains. That study can provide you with new ideas or a starting point for the flaws and problems you might want to give to your own villains.

New villains of all types continue to arrive on the scene—in movies, on television programs and in real life. Just when we think we have seen everything, a new evil personality or creature with a different or unique method of carrying out evil deeds appears.

Large creatures such as dinosaurs or overgrown apes have always made great foes for movie heroes to conquer, but a swirling fog can be just as frightening if the main characters don't know what's in it or how to make it go away.

CREATING A GREAT VILLAIN • 17

Snakes at any time can be frightening, but put a poisonous variety on a plane... over the ocean... and then let them lose... well, the result sold a lot of movie tickets.

Writers constantly seek new villains to do damage to the world or wreak havoc on the people around them. *You* might be the writer to develop the next imaginative villain who is out to rule the world or to take control of the small town and its immediate environs. New villains can appear at any time, in any form. Often writers may go back to classic literature, fables, legends or lore, or even the Bible, to find or shape new villainous personalities for movies, books or television programs. Is there a villain more evil than Satan?

As we help you develop your own villains and their nasty traits, this is a good time to remind you of some who have made their marks in literature, television, movies, comic books and in real life. At times, those real-life villains and their deeds can be even more frightening than the fictional villains that live only in our imagination.

The following list of villains from movies, television programs and books may contain many of the names or creatures you instantly remember, but as you study them, you can also see they are complex characters without an easy answer to why they eventually became the villains we love to hate.

Darth Vader – As the Dark Lord of the evil Empire in the *Star Wars* series, he was the arch-enemy of the rebels because he did whatever the Emperor told him to do without regard for life. But he began life as Anakin Skywalker until he turned to the Dark Side, thinking he could save Padme from death. Losing her and losing his limbs turned him into a mechanical monster with little regard for life.

Hannibal Lecter – Dr. Lecter was a smart man who enjoyed playing mind games with authority figures, especially law enforcement officials. But he was also a serial murderer who cooked up many of his victims into elaborate meals before he ate them.

Dracula – As a creature who could exist forever if he stayed out of the sunlight, he needed to exist on the blood of others. But he could also be quite suave and bewitch women to the point of wanting to give up their lives for him.

Lord Voldemort – As the arch-villain in the *Harry Potter* series, Lord Voldemort's desire was one of overwhelming domination and being the most powerful man in the world. The powers of young Harry Potter could hold him back, so Voldemort was determined to destroy him long before Harry could recognize and learn the sheer force of his magical gifts.

President Snow – As the despotic ruler in *The Hunger Games* stories, he is described by heroine Katniss as smelling like blood and roses. The blood came from bloody sores in his mouth, while the scent of roses came from the rose he wore in his lapel to hide the scent of blood.

Professor Moriarty – While he is recognized as a major villain in the literary world, he appeared in only a couple of Arthur Conan Doyle's *Sherlock Holmes* stories. That shows how much of an impact he made on readers. He was described as ruthless, highly intelligent and a mastermind of criminal activity.

The Joker – Batman's adversary craved power, but he also had a wicked sense of humor that he used as the driving force behind some of his crazier antics.

The Wicked Witch of the West – As portrayed in the popular movie, she was a bad witch who wanted to enslave the populace of the world of Oz. She had her own flying band of monkey henchmen who did as she directed.

Phantom of the Opera – Disfigured from birth, his undying love for a beautiful woman was what drove him. He taught Christine Daae to sing his opera music and wanted her to stay and live with him in his dark underworld. To achieve that, he was willing to steal, cheat and murder.

Real Life Villains

Villains are not confined to comic books, movies or television programs. Throughout human history a variety of men and women have done terrible things and proven to be real-life villains with the power of life or death or making life miserable for their fellow human beings. There have been mass-murdering dictators and rulers, sociopathic religious leaders, insane serial killers or greedy and pathologic politicians. All may steal from others or cheat without any sort of conscience or worrying about the consequences of their actions. They may also kill and maim for their own evil purposes. Knowing about some of these villains or studying who they were or the things they did in their lifetime can provide any writer with ideas for *their* works of fiction. Consider a few of the most memorable true-life villains over time, including some from recent years:

Roman Emperor Nero
Attila the Hun
Adolf Hitler
Josef Mengele
Charles Manson
Jim Jones
Ted Bundy
Timothy McVeigh
Osama Bin Laden
Bernie Madoff

It is interesting to note that all these men truly believed they were invincible, and that their way was the right way. Although Bundy and Manson killed others for the fun of it, Jim Jones truly believed his religious views were God-given. When he and the other leaders of his religious sect faced exposure by Congressman Leo Ryan and a group of inspectors in 1978, Jones turned a peaceful jungle colony into a village of mass death. Fearing exposure, he ordered the murders of the delegation which had been sent by concerned relatives to check on the circumstances and conditions of their families living at Jonestown. He also directed his men to gun down the group members who were trying to leave. Finally, Jones led his followers in a mass suicide that resulted in the deaths of hundreds of men, women and children.

American terrorist, Timothy McVeigh, committed the Oklahoma City bombing to prove a political point about the federal raid at Ruby Ridge, Texas. He and his cohorts ended up killing dozens of innocent children in a daycare center for federal employees.

Banker Bernie Madoff was not a killer, but he stole millions of dollars from investors who trusted him. His illegal actions resulted in financial ruin and several suicides for some people who lost their money to his crooked financial schemes.

Serial killings, while generally attributed to men, are not committed only by that sex. Some women can also be unbelievably cruel and claim many victims:

> Queen Mary I
> Lizzie Borden
> Aileen Wuornos
> Manson Follower- Susan Atkins
> Dorothea Puente

Female serial killer Aileen Wuornos was convicted of murdering six men along Florida freeways. She was sentenced to death and eventually executed in 2002. Susan Atkins and Patricia Krenwinkel chose to follow evil mastermind, Charles Manson, and helped in the bloody murders of the La Bianca family only days after killing six people, including pregnant actress, Sharon Tate. Another female Manson follower, Squeaky Fromme, wasn't arrested in those murders but later attempted to kill President Gerald Ford. All of those women remain in prison after 40+ years--Susan Atkins until her death in 2009.

There were also the real-life mothers, like Susan Smith, who killed their own children in the bathtub or in a lake. Some women, like Dorothea Puente, were nurses who murdered their elderly patients. The motive was to steal money from their victims.

One only has to turn on a daily newscast to find a real-life villain, whether it's a crooked politician whose daily lies attempt to fool the public, a ruthless business person out to defraud customers, or a parent who has murdered a family for selfish or financial reasons. Some cable networks carry regular crime programs about real-life murders or criminal activities with villains of all ages.

The world of fiction also continues to deliver new villains. New, evil and unique villainous characters are only as far away as our nearest library, bookstore, or movie theater. They even come into our homes on new television programs or in video games.

Studying fictional and real villains not only can provide an author with new inspiration for writing new stories, but it can also illustrate there are few boundaries that have not already been crossed at some point.

You can create *your* own villain for your specific story in any manner that works best for you and the story. A unique villain can help you create an unforgettable story. To quote an old saying, "the sky's the limit." *You* can create *your* own kind of villains *your* way to carry out whatever dastardly deeds you need him/her/it to accomplish. The more creative you are in your thinking, the better your villains will become. While some types have been used repeatedly, you might be the person who develops a completely new strain of villain. Turn on your imagination and see what sort of evil you can concoct to put into a villain.

Well-Known Villains from Fact & Fiction

Al Capone — Mob leader
Adolf Hitler – Dictator
Genghis Khan – Emperor
Smaug the dragon – Creature from *Lord of the Rings*
Klingons – *Star Trek* series
Black Jack Randall – *Outlander* series

CHAPTER 3

The Importance of Villains

*The more successful the villain,
the more successful the picture.*
Alfred Hitchcock, Director

C reating a memorable villain for your story can be challenging and great fun, but is a villain necessary in your story?

YES!

Absolutely.

As we have noted, nearly every fictional story needs some sort of villain, whether real, alien, or imaginary. We've also mentioned that a natural catastrophe, a disease, or an idea or philosophy can also serve as the villain.

While heroes and heroines are the backbone for any tale, villains give stories that extra touch, which can bring out the best and worst in our main characters. Heroes and heroines are like the meat and sauce in the stew, but villains provide the spice--that extra bite to the senses that keeps you coming back for seconds and makes every story a little different or unique.

For a story to be remembered, the author needs someone or something that seeks to prevent the protagonist from reaching his or her goal, no matter how large or small that goal is.

Let's look at the structure of most works of popular fiction. In order for the story to sell, it has to have a purpose. In order to have that purpose, **the main character must have a goal**. S/he has to have one of the following to solve, overcome or change:

> A personal problem so urgent that he/she is forced to find a way to fix it
>
> A dilemma that he/she must solve or unravel, or his/her life or family is doomed
>
> A sticky situation that has to be remedied or his/her life or the lives of loved ones will go down the drain
>
> A life-threatening obstacle or personal problem that must be handled immediately
>
> A decision that could affect the future
>
> A dangerous situation or person threatening him/her or the family

Without an adequate villain, suitable for the genre you have chosen, the main character will solve the problem without delay, or negate the dilemma easily, or find a simple solution or conqueror all the obstacles immediately and **there will not be much of a story.**

Let's put it another way and take that goal back one more step. No one wants to read a story where everything is great and the world is perfect while everyone is the same and does the same thing every day. No, we want problems in our stories. We want characters who might start out as ordinary or quirky or who might start out ordinary and then become true heroes when they are faced with adversity. We want something to happen, whether the event is unusual or earth-shattering. We might even have heroes who are larger than life, but then they will suddenly be challenged. Why? Because we want our characters in stories to learn and grow. Once the story starts and characters are introduced, something must occur that will change, endanger or disrupt a character's normal life. We then need the characters to try to get their lives back or to choose to move forward in a positive manner. We have those characters—now they must learn and grow.

To achieve that goal, your main character must immediately run into some kind of a problem or a situation that needs fixing within the first pages of your book or story, even if it is just unhappiness with a boring life! We want the lives of the main characters to change from their ordinary world early in the story. It doesn't matter what the problem is.

It could be a decision for a better life or it could be the search for a suddenly missing document. It might even be a discovery of a map to a treasure from the past. It could also be something as simple as the character wanting to move up in the company, but someone is standing in his/her way. And then that person ends up dead. Or it might be as simple as a character trying to decide if he/she wants to go away to school or stay close to home.

But even a decision to stay close to home could develop into a catastrophe if the decision is forced because someone killed the hero's mother and he must become a parent to his younger brothers and sisters. Even a vacation that is scheduled to get away from a tedious life can turn into an exciting adventure.

Whatever your main character's goal is, even if it is to lead a simple life, your villain is going to come along and throw a monkey wrench into the whole situation.

In other words, to start off any story your main character must encounter some kind of a problem that suddenly occurs and needs fixing. It doesn't really matter what the problem is. It could be:

> Find the killer who murdered someone close to the hero/heroine
>
> Locate the missing person
>
> Find the lost treasure, fabled city, valuable artifact
>
> Help a brother get away from a gang
>
> Stop drinking and start a new life
>
> Move to a new neighborhood, city, or a new country
>
> A spooky new neighbor moves in next door
>
> Getting into college or making new friends

Whatever the problem might be, it should revolve around the protagonist's GOAL in the story. Once that goal is set, obstacles will begin appearing that might hold the hero/heroine back or challenge him/her in some way. The job of the villain is to keep the hero/heroine from achieving that goal. If there is no goal, or no villain, there is no story.

As the author, your job is to make certain the protagonist has a challenging enough problem to tackle. Then you should make certain the villain is strong enough to fight its achievement.

As we have noted, the villain doesn't have to be a person. Evil can be a villain all by itself and so can many natural forces. The key to the villains' role is that they or it must be ruthless and relentless. A virus or a volcano may not have a personal motive, but its drive is aimed at destruction, and that makes it a challenging opposing force for the hero or heroine.

It (or the villain) may not be conquered by the end of your story, but the hero/heroine must find a way out or to survive the villainous onslaught. Let's look at some more examples of villains and why they might make such memorable foes.

The movie, *Fargo,* has a whole cast of villains, starting with car dealer Carl Lundegaard. He wants his wife kidnapped and the movie opens with him hiring two petty crooks (villains) to take her captive. At least he thinks they are just thieves. One turns out to be a cold-blooded killer, and the second may be inept, but he is also quick-tempered and willing to kill in retaliation if angered.

On the other side of the equation, the story is about the heroine, Sheriff Marge Gunderson. Her calm, simple life in Fargo is complicated by the grisly murders of a highway patrolman and two innocent travelers. She just wants to do her daily job and have her baby. Without those murders, her biggest problems might be where to have lunch in Fargo and dealing with morning sickness. Instead, she is forced to drive to Minneapolis, where she eventually realizes Lundegaard's duplicity, and then must confront the killer in a gun battle.

In the book and movie, *Silence of the Lambs,* we also get multiple villains. Buffalo Bill had a well in his house where he could keep his victims until he murdered them, skinned them and turned them into clothing. But he wasn't as frightening as Hannibal Lecter who helped to track him down. Lecter bragged to FBI agent Clarice Starling about killing his victims and serving them up for dinner.

Even a calm neighborhood, where everyone knows everyone else, can harbor villains of all types. A teenage girl's disappearance sets the stage for the intrigue and violence of Dennis Lehane's book, *Mystic River.* Three former childhood friends, Sean, Jimmy and Dave, find themselves thrown back together as adults when Jimmy's daughter is found murdered. Dave becomes a suspect when he comes home covered in blood and can't remember the previous night's events. Sean is the detective who must solve the case. But *who* is the *real* villain in this case? Jimmy is ready to take the law into his own hands against his childhood friend.

Mother nature can flood a neighborhood or threaten a volcanic eruption and become a villain that man can tame, but not defeat. The human villains in this type of story might be the people who are so focused on their own survival that they are willing to sacrifice humanity so their family gets away, including taking the only truck in town loaded with their own possessions rather than helping families who have no way to get out. Other villains in this story might include town leaders who ignored warnings of the dam breaking or the volcanic eruption so they could continue to profit from land sales.

Society's values often cause trouble through differences in classes and ethical outlooks. Bankers who would throw out needy families rather than give them more time to pay a mortgage or get a new job can become villains as can poor swindlers who move into a property where they don't intend to pay rent.

Society itself might have been considered a villain in Thomas Wolfe's bestselling book, *Bonfire of the Vanities,* where a wrong turn by the hero, Sherman McCoy, turns his life as a Wall Street guru upside down. When he ends up on trial in a well-publicized hit-and-run case, where everyone around him is out for themselves, the battle for justice puts his life and his privileged lifestyle into question. Villains of all kinds come forward to make his life more miserable as the story twists and turns in a variety of directions until the reader discovers the truth.

As we have illustrated, villains can come in all sizes and shapes. Animals, beasts, creatures or machines can make great villains, especially if they have superpowers like Hal in *A Space Odyssey*. Without this computer's presence and actions, the story would have been simply a space journey.

The movie, *Alien,* another space adventure, was also defined by its villain. That story of a space ship crew locked aboard with an alien that dripped acid would have been different if the stowaway was *E.T.* That little space creature just wanted to phone home. In its case, the villains of the story were the scientists who wanted to keep E.T. on earth to be studied.

A particularly monstrous villain can also draw audiences and keep them returning. Why has *King Kong* been re-made so many times? Why do those dinosaurs from *Jurassic Park* keep coming back?

The *Alien* creature had the worst intentions – to lure space ships to a planet and kill the humans on board, then commandeer space ships to keep moving to other worlds. This villain proved so popular its nasty presence became the focal point of several sequels. Don't underestimate the power of your villains. A unique or noteworthy villain can be as popular in new stories as the heroes themselves.

Some elements of creating a worthy villain are similar for aspiring authors. The villain's presence should be felt early in the story. Villains usually provide the catalyst for the hero and/or heroine. Once the villain makes his/her/its presence known, the storyline or life is going to change for the main characters. The focus of the story will be on how to bring that villain down, even if your main characters don't know who the villain is or what it is or any motive involved. All the heroes and heroines will know is that their world has changed, and they must begin to try to reclaim a normal life by figuring out who or what is causing all their sudden problems and then how to get rid of it to go back to the normal world.

The main characters might be simply trying to bring an end to the problem itself. Your hero or heroine might simply want to get their normal world back by exposing the villain, rather than totally destroying it, depending on the genre of your book. We'll look at how to develop different villains for different genres in a later chapter. But whatever the choice, the constant presence of the villain is going to prevent a return to normalcy or to move forward to a better life for the hero or heroine.

Few authors do that better than Stephen King did in his book, *Misery*. In this story, the famous writer is driving back to the city when he gets into an accident and is taken in by villain, Annie Wilkes, his self-declared most fervent fan. But instead of hours of hero worship as he heals, she discovers his plans for her favorite character, and she doesn't like them one bit. She goes from being his savior to his captor who is willing to go to any length, including murder, to make him write the story she wants. As the savior turned villain, she is determined to keep him captive until he follows her wishes.

Would there have been a *Misery* story without that villain? The author, Paul Sheldon, would have simply either been cared for by a kind stranger or an ambulance would have been called for him. He would have gone back to his writing while Annie Wilkes would have been just another unsatisfied reader when she eventually got a copy of the book he had been intending to write.

Stephen King does a good job of making his villains extra spooky and unique. We're never quite sure what is haunting the Overlook Hotel in his bestseller, *The Shining*, but its supernatural presence in the Colorado mountain hotel has kept people captive there or driven them crazy on numerous occasions.

We also never learn who or what the real villain is in *The Stand*, other than a supernatural force, even though it is embodied in The Walking Dude, Randall Flagg. The story begins with a virus that decimates the world and results in separate camps of humans who eventually battle it out in Las Vegas for the very soul of the remaining people in the world.

These are the sorts of villains you can construct for your stories, based on what you want your main characters to do in the book. You can decide how your plot will challenge the heroes and heroines through the villains, whether it is a person, a spaceship, a virus or an unknown force.

Romance novelist, Joan Wilder, in *Romancing the Stone*, was a popular author to her fans, but she didn't realize how resourceful and capable she was until she was forced to make a trip to South America to save her sister. When a bus accident leaves her stranded, she hires Jack to help get her through the jungle, but she soon discovers how capable she really is – swinging across a deep ravine and confronting armed gunmen. In the end she must save her own life in a confrontation with the villain, Colonel Zolo, and she returns to New York as a hopeful, rather than hopeless, romantic.

As the author, you can decide if your villain will actually start out as the heroic do-gooder and then transform into someone evil as the story goes along. You might even have your villain be a hero in one book and then turn villain later. In the original *Star Wars* movies, we met Darth Vader as an established villain. Only later did George Lucas come back and bring us the story of the young Anakin Skywalker who began as a youthful hero who wanted to become a pilot.

After becoming strong and learning the ways of the Jedi, his course began to change. With the death of his mother and filled with growing fears about his wife, he began to turn bitter. Eventually he turned against his friends and the Force. Rejecting his former life and companions, he fell into the clutches of the evil Emperor who was feeding his hate.

Moviegoers were shown the trials that caused the eventual transformation from the role of a hero to that of an almost mechanical villain ready to do the bidding of the evil Emperor. As he lay alone burning, having lost an arm and his legs we could understand why Anakin might feel abandoned. In those dramatic scenes of the second trilogy, he went from being the pilot/father with such hope to the villainous Darth Vader. His transformation was complete.

Your heroic main characters might also be like the tormented Jack Torrance in *The Shining* who went from the hero trying to help his family to the murderous villain out to kill them. His wife, Wendy, went from being someone just trying to get through the winter to the heroine who has to fight for her life and save her son.

The heroine might also be a common man or woman character, such as Ripley, the strong lone survivor in *Alien*. She had to channel extra strength to meet the final challenge and get rid of the alien creature once and for all. In the first installment, she was simply another crew member. In later movies we saw her as a strong heroine who had beaten the alien once and knew what she was up against. In those later movies she was known as a leader, but in the first episode she was simply another crew person without special characteristics.

Sheriff Martin Brody was uncertain about life on his small island and didn't like water in *Jaws,* but by the end, he had conquered the shark and was happily paddling back to shore, having discovered unknown strengths he didn't realize he possessed at the beginning of the movie and book. Great villains can make great heroes out of the ordinary people who vanquish them.

Heroes can come in all shapes and sizes, but they grow and become stronger by defeating the villain, such as Brody in *Jaws* or Sheriff Marge Gunderson in *Fargo.* They might start out as a superhero, like *Batman,* but as you create either, consider who will be on the other side of the equation.
A strong villain will require a stronger hero or heroine or someone who becomes stronger over the course of the novel.

Make your stories more involving and increase the tension by giving both your heroes and your villains qualities that make them fight a fierce battle against each other that makes the reader want to keep turning the pages.

Just as with your heroes and heroines, villains will come in all shapes and sizes as well, but they certainly can't be—or shouldn't be--ignored, as the crazed lover shouted in the movie, *Fatal Attraction.*

Without villains, there would be no need for heroes because we would not need them to save us from the bad guys.

The bottom line is that both the hero and the villain are necessary to your books and screenplays. Whether you choose to use a person, an animal, a government or a virus, make your villains fit your story and then let your imagination run wild.

Necessary Villains

    Colonel Zolo – *Romancing the Stone*
    The Shark – *Jaws*
    Randall Flagg – *The Stand*
    The Ancient One – *Phantoms*
    The Emperor – *Star Wars – Return of the Jedi*

CHAPTER 4

Creating Your Villain

*Villains are meant to be black hearted in popular novels.
If you say I have a grey hearted villain, then I've failed.*
Ken Follett, Author

Discovering and unveiling the perfect villain for your story is as critical as finding or creating the perfect hero or heroine. It is hard to imagine a more perfect villain than Hannibal Lecter from *Silence of the Lambs*, or *Red Dragon*, but he wasn't the actual villain in either story. Other serial killers were the villains. Clarice Starling in *Lambs* and Will Graham in *Dragon* were simply getting information from him. But Hannibal the Cannibal has all the perfect attributes of a bad guy and he was already in jail for his own crimes. As a result of his popularity in those books, he would soon star in his own story, as well as several movies. Godzilla started out terrorizing Tokyo but before he was finished, he ended up fighting off other creatures who were threatening humanity.

As you create the perfect villains for your books, you need to consider their roles in your stories. As we noted earlier, Annie Wilkes was the perfect villain for *Misery*. No other reader, except someone as obsessed as Annie, would have kept Paul Sheldon captive or put a writer through such "misery."

The villain in *Pride and Prejudice*, Mr. Wickham, was just the sort of person all the young women of the Bennet family desired--handsome, witty and an officer. Unlike the cold, proud Mr. Darcy, Wickham could charm the ladies, from young, innocent teenage Lydia up to Mrs. Bennet. He was the perfect villain to draw them all in with his lies, until they discovered the truth about him.

The key to deciding who or what will be the villain of your story depends on what genre you are writing and to what level you need a villain. If you are writing a sweet romance, the villain might be as simple as the evil rival who is trying to come between your hero and heroine or a charming ne'er do well like Wickham who is trying to win the hand of the heroine for her money. It could also be a troublesome mother or friend who might eventually realize the wrong he or she is doing and then changes to help the couple eventually come together. Not every villain will necessarily need to be destroyed at the end of the story, though that person might need a lesson in diplomacy or might need to leave the hero and heroine alone in the future.

Each individual plot should determine the strength and the struggle caused by the villain, but as the author you need to be the directing force. Even if you are writing a sweet romance, that villain needs to be strong enough to be a formidable force or obstacle that might be keeping the couple apart or causing problems for either the hero or heroine. You don't want a struggle that could be won on page ten unless you're writing a short story. In that case, the villain could be as simple as something like a deadly sin, such as greed. Scrooge needed to learn in "A Christmas Carol" that the people around him were more valuable than his wealth or making money. It was a simple life's lesson, but it was one he had not learned through many years of living and one he needed to learn before he died.

But greed is an idea, and while you can use a concept as a villain in a short story, such as "A Christmas Carol," you are more likely to have a person or something more complex and complete as your villain in a novel. Even in the short story, though, there is the need to create characters to embody the idea of greed. The character of Jacob Marley is a good example of what and who Scrooge had become in the villainous sense, and his presence shows where Scrooge might end up if he doesn't change his life.

With that in mind, let's look at how you should go about creating the perfect villain for your own story:

Make the villain personal to each story and its main characters. In modern romances, the villain can be anyone, so selecting specific looks and characteristics are completely open to your imagination. In the movie, *Working Girl*, Sigourney Weaver plays the part of Katharine and is everything the heroine, Melanie Griffith as Tess, aspires to be. Then Tess learns the truth about Kate - that underneath this aggressive executive is a back-stabbing bitch. She makes a wonderful villain who "gets" hers in the end. In this case, there is a definite contrast in the looks of the two different characters and that is the sort of information you want to keep in mind as you design the different characters. Katharine had a more confident air than her underling, and her style and demeanor showed that. Her speech, her style of dress, her manner was that of a confident woman. On the other hand, Tess was less confident and dressed in a less formal style. The seemingly "perfect" Katharine made just the right villain.

In some love stories, the "villain" is the attitude or belief the main character harbors. This inner emotional problem keeps the lovers apart until the characters learn how to change, control or adjust the "villain" or bad trait. Perhaps the heroine is overly jealous. While the villain may appear to be her rival, it could turn out that the heroine simply needs to learn to deal with her jealousy instead. By making the perceived villain a perfectly sweet character who eventually teaches the heroine the lesson about jealousy, the story not only teaches a lesson, but makes a comment on perceptions as well.

Your villain can provide a challenge to your main characters.

As we have noted, for a story to be successful, the main character needs to face a challenge, but he/she also needs to face conflict. A story with a character who sets out with a goal and immediately achieves it isn't going to be as fun to read as a story featuring a character with the odds stacked against him/her. A story featuring obstacles and various twists and turns as the character grows in strength is going to be even more engrossing.

For years, fiction readers and movie fans have been chilled by the forbidding villain, Mrs. Danvers, the housekeeper, in *Rebecca*. She tried to make the heroine go crazy with her talk of how perfect the dead Rebecca was. In some ways, Rebecca was the ultimate villain in this story with her lies and her deceitful behavior. But Mrs. Danvers was the perfect villain to battle with the young heroine, the new lady of Manderley. While we don't get to know much of the heroine's background, we do know she was a companion serving older, wealthy women. The cold, proper, demanding Mrs. Danvers was exactly the sort of person who would and could intimidate the young heroine, as was the absent Rebecca. The dead woman's presence lurked around Manderley in the form of remaining clothes, her old stationery, and in all the choices she had made in running the estate. Mrs. Danvers kept that presence alive as she tormented the young, new mistress.

Your villain's appearance and demeanor may demonstrate a contrast. In addition to the mental and personality differences between your villains and heroes/heroines, you might also keep the physical attributes of your characters in mind as you create your heroes, heroines and villains. Providing a physical contrast between the main character and the villain can make hero or heroine more sympathetic. How many times have readers enjoyed stories of the skinny, physically untrained hero who ends up defeating the muscular, domineering villain? How about stories of a smart, thinking woman who overthrows a bullying overlord?

Physical differences provide a visual difference that readers can imagine and respond to. Is she tall and gangly with wispy hair while the woman who is her competitor is shorter with feminine curves and always well-coiffed? Is your heroine always worried that she has a stain on her skirt or fighting wild untamable hair while the villain is always impeccably dressed and immaculately coiffed?

What about the villain's confidence level? Does she speak with a measured, cultured tone while the heroine feels like her voice is high, squeaky and nasal?

Building a contrast between your secondary characters, your villain and your main characters can also be useful to enhance comparisons among them all. This could be even more important when dealing with a mystery where your protagonist is searching for the villain. Each person will be a little different, but only one difference will count—who and why the person committed the crime. Think of a story like Agatha Christie's *Murder on the Orient Express*. Discovering the answer to the identity of the killer did not necessarily answer the question of who was the real villain of the story.

If you use character sheets or written descriptions to create your characters, once you have decided what you want your hero or heroine to look like, pull up another character sheet and go through the same sort of checklist for your villains. The better you know your villain the more real he/she/it will become to you and the more real you can make the villain for your readers.

Of course, the choice of your villain's appearance and how he, she or it will function is determined in good part by the sort of story or genre of book you write. A science fiction story can mean anything from aliens to dinosaurs as villains. A romance can contain a villain who is anything from a jealous ex-wife to a disease that is threatening a loved one to an attitude that is threatening the romance.

As you create your villain, you will want to keep all these factors in mind. Exactly who or what is your villain? Is your villain a human male or female? Will a woman or man be more of a challenge to your hero or heroine? Does the gender even matter or are you more likely to use an alien, such as the space travelers in the movie, *Independence Day?* What about the machine Hal 9000 in the movie *2001 - A Space Odyssey?* The human-eating plant Audrey II in *Little Shop of Horrors* was a creature from outer space. Captain Ahab's nemesis, Moby Dick, gave him and his ship's crew a merry chase while the shark in *Jaws* threatened a whole town and its way of life. A bigger question in *Moby Dick* was whether the whale was the villain or was it the obsessed Captain Ahab who got most of his crew killed while he pursued the whale.

A creature, zombies or shapeshifter of some kind can also be a threat as Stephen King has shown us time after time. Evil can even be a big old hotel with a bunch of ghosts inhabiting it. Remember the terror he brought us in *The Shining?* Or in the short story, *The Mist?* In Dean Koontz's book, *Phantoms,* all we knew was that the enemy was "the Ancient One." We never saw it appear in the book, although its presence was all around.

As you can see, the type of villain you choose will probably depend on the genre of your work. If you are writing fantasy or science fiction, then the sky is the limit. You can have any or all of the types of villains listed above or you can create new villains that have never been seen previously.

No matter what type of villain you decide to use, you will still need to figure out its limits or if it has any. The Wicked Witch in *The Wizard of Oz* appeared to be invincible to the people of Oz, and even to Dorothy when they met. But in their final confrontation, we all learned that she'd had one weakness all along – she could be destroyed with water. The same was true of the aliens in *Signs*.

As the villains' creator, the power of their strengths and weaknesses is up to you as you write your stories. You get to make up their strengths and weaknesses, but you should know them as you begin to write your story. Making notes on your villain—their strengths and weaknesses, their form of communication, the way they live—all these elements will help you keep your story and plot straight while you are writing the book. If you make a sudden discovery or change a part of the villain while writing, be certain to go back and put that into your notes. You don't want to have mentioned your creature is impervious to water in an early paragraph and then use it as a destructive force later. Those are the types of mistakes readers will discover and mention in reviews.

If you're writing romance, mystery, western, young adult or comedy, your villain will probably be human, so once you decide on your villain, you have more things to consider:

> What villain will look like - his/her physical appearance

What emotional qualities the villain might need to possess to make the plot work

What the villain's motivations are for causing havoc with the protagonist

What possible weaknesses the villain might have that the hero or heroine can discover or use

Using those guidelines, let's begin building our villain from the outside to the inside. We will figure out their emotional baggage and motivations later as we examine their role in the story, but first let's handle the basics of physical appearance.

Creating a character, whether good or bad, can be like a drawing a picture. You start with a few lines here and there to form a basic outline of the scene, but then you continue to fill in the details until the picture comes fully into focus.

Physical Appearance

Your villain can't really come alive until YOU know what he/she/it looks like. You can make your villain anything you want—from a handsome banker to a gorgeous actress to an ugly misfit, or the villain can be as plain and ordinary as the boy or girl next door. The bottom line is you have the choice of designing your villain almost any way, but you must make that villain a complete person or entity in order to make him or her come alive for the reader.

For example, if you are writing a sweet romance, you probably want the villain to be fairly normal, while if you are deep into a sci-fi or paranormal fantasy, anything goes. However, even in a romance, your villain doesn't have to *look* normal. Perhaps an accident disfigured the villain and because of that accident, he/she holds the hero/heroine responsible and sets out to either destroy your protagonist or destroy the relationship she is trying to have. Perhaps the villain feels she will never have love and because the heroine destroyed her chance at love, she won't let her have it either. Maybe the villain is so glamorous the drab police heroine fears she is going after the woman because of her looks and thus misses several vital clues.

To develop your villains, you can begin as you might create any other character in the book. Start with a list of the basics and fill in as much as necessary, or consider writing a short descriptive paragraph about that character. Do whatever works best for you.

Since we need to know what the character or creature looks like, a good beginning might be to include what is normally found on a driver's license. Even if you are writing a fantasy villain or a space creature, an overall physical description is necessary so that you can verbally paint a picture for the reader. The best policy is to fill in the following blanks:

Height:

Weight:

Hair Color:

Eye Color:

Build: (thin, stocky, curvy, etc.)

Distinguishing Characteristics:

This is a simple list, but the reason we recommend it as a starting point is because it allows you to go in any direction necessary. From here you can give your villains any form or substance you want. Are they a creature with scales and green eyes? Or a soft, mindless, mushy piece of slime that consumes everything and everyone in its path? Is it a creature or a person? As noted above, you can either fill out this list or write a paragraph of description, but you need to know the appearance of your villain.

You can start filling out this list at any point, but Distinguishing Characteristics might be the most important element on this list. If you are dealing with a creature, that might be the place to begin. If you are dealing with a person, it might also be the place you list any special reason the villain might have a grudge against the protagonist.

Perhaps the villain has a disfigurement from an accident caused by the hero or his/her family. Perhaps the hero's brother beat out the villain in a special competition. You might also list any special charms that villain might display to disarm the hero or heroine. Perhaps he is a math genius trying to prove himself smarter than anyone and the hero requests help in solving a series of problems or perhaps the villain is trying to outsmart police and offers his services. The distinguishing characteristic might also be the weak point that allows the hero to save the day.

While knowing the villain's looks will make the villain become more visually alive, you will still need to dig a little deeper into the motivation behind that villain's antics and that can also be part of a villain's special characteristics. Just as no two villains are going to look alike, they won't think alike either, and their motivations will vary as much as your heroes and heroines.

Emotional Qualities

The villain's specific emotional makeup can play a major role in your story. In many ways, these character qualities are more important than what a villain looks like because they will determine HOW your villain is going to act in any given situation.

How does your villain enjoy his/her acts of cruelty? Is the villain a sadist who likes to see those around him/her suffer?

Is he a shrewd businessman who plans his dirty deeds carefully ahead of time? Or does she display a charismatic personality as a charming sociopath?

Perhaps he is cunning and sly or unstable and brooding. Think of all the psychological problems people have and then list the negative characteristics you might want to give your villain to make the plot work.

Does he carry a grudge for something the hero once did to him? Is she jealous of everything the heroine gets because she feels she is smarter or prettier and thinks she deserves it instead? Were they childhood rivals where the hero/heroine always got his/her way and now the villain wants to get revenge?

Are the hero and villain competitors currently battling it out in the corporate world for a top position after being college students where one feels the other cheated?

Is he a hard-working husband worried that the friendly stay-at-home dad next door is out to steal his wife? Which one will turn out to be the hero and which will be the villain? Emotional fears such as jealousy, greed, frustration, or irrational distrust can all trigger emotional reactions that can turn a normally rational person into an angry villain out to destroy the hero or heroine.

Setting Motivation

Once you have decided on the emotional characteristics of your villains, you still need to decide WHY they are acting as they do in your story. Your reasons should be personal to the villain, but that doesn't necessarily translate to a personal grudge against the hero or heroine. Your villain could be battling humanity at large, like inventing a deadly virus or robbing a bank. Perhaps the villain attacks someone close to the hero. Since your story is about your hero or heroine, the villain might be trying to achieve his or her goals simply for himself, but then the hero gets in the way of what the villain wants. As we noted earlier, eventually the story becomes the battle between the hero and villain, but it doesn't always need to begin that way.

If your villain sets out to destroy a city or take control of the town, it could be that the hero steps forward and then tries to stop him. At that point it becomes the personal battle between the hero and villain. That was the situation in both of the movies *Die Hard* and *Die Hard Two*. The villains had predetermined targets, but police officer John McClane got in the way and the battle became a personal struggle between him and the criminal masterminds. In the first, the villain and his gang were trying to steal a fortune in securities that were in a bank vault in the building they took over. In the second movie, the villains were trying to free a drug kingpin. In both cases, McClane's personal reason for fighting the villains was trying to save his wife. In the first, she had been taken hostage and when her boss was killed, she became the leader of the hostages. In the second, she was on a plane trying to fly into the airport the villains had taken over as they tried to get the kingpin out of the country. The result was plenty of explosive action but the basis behind both was McClane's drive to save his wife. The hero's motive was personal.

A family member or a loved one in danger is always a good motive for your hero or heroine, no matter what kind of villain he or she faces. In many thrillers or action movies, the problem boils down to one or two characters the hero is trying to save.

Of course, a hero or heroine's job can also play a role in him/her becoming the star of the story. A police officer or a military person might automatically become the hero or heroine of a book or movie if that person is the commanding officer or gets put in charge. Jeff Goldblum played David Levinson, a cable TV worker, who discovered the secret code being used by the aliens in *Independence Day*, while Will Smith played Captain Steven Hillier, an Air Force pilot who captured an alien. Together they became the heroes who join forces with the President played by Bill Pullman to defeat the alien villains. Perhaps the most unlikely hero in that movie was the drunken crop-dusting pilot played by Randy Quaid. A former pilot in the Vietnam War, he gave his life to blow up one of the main spaceships. His reason? It was the same as the other heroes in the movie – they wanted to save the world, but more importantly, they wanted to save their families.

On the other hand, the villain can have just about any personal motive he or she wants. How do you come up with workable motives for your villains? Look to their flaws and weaknesses or a combination of both. We have a good starting point that stretches back in time that can be very useful whenever you need to look for a good reason a nasty villain might act in a certain way. If you're looking for motives to create villains or for traits that you can give them to make them come across even worse in your stories, consider their flaws or you might go back in time to the Seven Deadly Sins:

1. Pride
2. Lust
3. Greed
4. Sloth
5. Gluttony
6. Envy
7. Wrath

Villains have been given these flaws or traits as far back in time as storytellers have been creating tales. If you're looking for a nasty quality for your villain or for a motive for why they are doing bad things, you need look no farther than this list. From Satan to President Snow in *Hunger Games* to Darth Vader in the *Star Wars* series, villains fall victims to these flaws. Edmond Dantes in *The Count of*

Monte Cristo has several of these "sins." Author Alexander Dumas combined wrath and pride in creating Dantes, making him very angry and then instilled him with pride and the need for revenge. Current audiences might see the same flaws in the science fiction character, Darth Vader.

Let's take a closer look at these flaws and how you can use them in your stories:

Pride is a trait that can be found as easily in a hero or heroine as it might be found in a villain, but it is definitely worse in a villain. Pride was the problem Mr. Darcy had to overcome before he could win Elizabeth in *Pride and Prejudice*.

Lust is a flaw that can turn a normally quiet, calm person into a crazed villain. Writers have used it for years in suspense stories or thrillers. It is a trait that can make either a man or woman so obsessed that the person will rob banks for love, kidnap children to prove one's love or start a ghastly, murderous rampage to get a loved one's attention.

There is probably no greater villain or villainess who illustrates the dangers of lust more than Alex Forrest, played superbly by actress Glenn Close in the 1987 movie, *Fatal Attraction*. That movie was enough to make any married man think twice about having an extramarital affair or even a one-night stand. She took lust and wrath to a whole new level, putting acid on his car, kidnapping his daughter and let's not forget her attack on that poor pet bunny.

Greed is another of those negative traits that can make for unforgettable villains. Who doesn't dream of winning the lottery or making it in the corporate community?

Greed was at the core of one of the greatest TV villains of all time. JR Ewing on the hit program, *Dallas,* was willing to risk everything and everyone around him for money and power. He was determined to be successful in the oil business, no matter who got hurt. He was one of those villains who was so unforgettable, viewers tuned in every week, just to see his next crooked exploit. The episode where he was shot and the later episode revealing the shooter remain among the most watched programs ever televised.

Gordon Gekko, the villain played by Michael Douglas, in the movie, *Wall Street,* had the saying "Greed is good," as his motto. His quest for power knew no bounds, and he nearly destroyed his son and his firm in his quest for money and power.

Sloth and Gluttony are also in the sin category and can be used to make your villains appear even more hideous. There is no better example than the evil Jabba the Hutt in the *Star Wars* series. He kept women and other captives locked in chains while he sat around and entertained himself and his followers with gladiator-like battles in his dark den of evil.

In *The Great Gatsby,* it is the indolent lifestyle of Daisy and Tom Buchanan that plays as much of a villainous role as the actual villain himself. In his drive to become part of the rich crowd, Jay Gatsby becomes a doomed man, consumed by not only what he wants, but what he cannot attain.

Envy of someone else's possessions, achievements, or personal qualities can turn a hero into a villain or make a villain do monstrous deeds. How many stories have you read where the "bad" guy is envious of the hero or heroine and does his best—or worst—to get what he wants? Think of the killer who wants to step into another's life to get that person's spouse and is willing to go to any lengths to do it.

Many teen movies or books have used envy to give life to their villains. Movies such as *Heathers, Mean Girls,* and *Cruel Intentions* featured villains who were so consumed by jealousy that they turned to dirty tricks to become popular or steal others' boyfriends away from them.

Wrath is always a great trait for villains. Anger can drive a sane man to commit terrible or evil deeds that the person might not consider doing otherwise. It was her sudden discovery of what author Paul Sheldon planned to do with her favorite character that drove Annie Wilkes into angry madness in *Misery*.
She went from being a caregiving nurse to a vengeful, torturing monster.

The Seven Deadly Sins have been used for as long as people have been telling or writing stories, and they probably will continue to be used long into the future. They not only can illustrate the worst in people, they can also lead to horrible consequences as we've seen in so many books, plays and movies over the years.

Lust for a man or woman has led many a hero and villain to lock horns over another man or woman such as Cal and Jack's love for Rose in *Titanic*. Gruber's greedy desire for money turned him into the villain in *Die Hard* and it was also the driving force in *Fargo*. Wrath over the fear he had been betrayed was what made Anakin Skywalker turn on the Jedis. Envy was the driving force that drove Snow White's evil stepmother to madness.

The bottom line is that if you ever find yourself in need of a motive for your villains, start by looking at the Seven Deadly Sins. They can provide a believable motivation for just about any sort of villain you decide to create.

Nonhuman Villains

We have been focused on creating human villains, or villains who can think, but there may be other villains you want to create who are not human.

If you are writing science fiction or fantasy, you may decide to use forces or entities that are nonhuman as your villains. You may also decide to use other societal rules or regulations as a villain. For instance, your western heroine may not only be facing the crooked sheriff with a grudge who interprets the law to his own desire, but she may also have to go up against the city or state law that prevents her from owning property in the developing West of the 1860s.

A hero and heroine might find they have moved their family into a small town with strange rules only to discover there is a monster prowling outside of town like a horde of zombies or a virus that is threatening the population and that is the reason for the strange laws.

Something as small as a virus can be a villain, but don't forget there may also be governments or government forces who can act as villains. In these cases, there may be a human counterpart to go up against the hero. The Evil Empire in the *Star Wars* movies was embodied in Darth Vader and the Emperor.

As you work on developing your villains, you may also want to consider the personality traits of your hero and heroine to decide how you might test them. Is your heroine too trusting? Perhaps she encounters a creature with a broken limb who might earn sympathy. The heroine feels sorry for the wounded creature so she unshackles the other limb. Then the seemingly-weak creature suddenly attacks her with the superhuman strength to escape. The heroine won't make that same mistake next time they meet.

Also keep in mind that even as your hero or heroine battles the outside threat, there may also be a person or other human villain who is encouraging or supporting the nonhuman villain. Author Robin Cook, who has written numerous medical thrillers, such as *Pandemic, Cell, Outbreak* and *Coma* often has his heroes and heroines not only battling a medical threat such as a deadly virus or medical threat but also villainous, unscrupulous doctors or drug companies with their own motives. In *Outbreak* he had a couple of army officers who were willing to destroy an entire town rather than admit to the government development of a viral weapon. In *Cell*, he used a smart phone app and health care companies as part of the villainous plot.

Don't shortchange the presence of a human villain even if you use non-human villains in your works. Remember, even vampires need a human counterpart who has to help them. Your job as an author when writing these kinds of horror or mystery books may be not only to determine how to defeat the villain but also how the human counterpart who is acting as the villain will be revealed. You must decide whether to destroy both and how it will be done.

From the very beginning chapter in the *Jurassic Park* series, the heroes and heroines have had to fight not only the huge and unpredictable villainous creatures, but the human villains who insist on bringing them into contact with people. So far, for the past twenty years, every attempt has resulted in chaos and carnage, but audiences and readers continue to respond and come back for more.

In Stephen King's novel, *The Shining,* the villain, Jack Torrance, has been destroyed, and the heroine, Wendy, and her son have escaped the horror of the evil Overlook Hotel, but the building remains and whatever ghosts or creatures or entities cause all the problems are

CREATING A GREAT VILLAIN • 53

not gone. They are simply waiting for their next round of victims who might be stranded at the hotel high in the Colorado Rocky Mountains.

Haunted houses and evil spells have proven their popularity many times over as the basis for creating villains that brave heroes and heroines must battle in short stories, books and movies.

If you are writing a series, where the hero or heroine faces a new villain in every book, some of these guidelines will be different, and we will look at creating villains for a series in a later chapter. You don't want your detective or scientist to keep battling a similar villain in each book. Yes, the monsters of *Jurassic Park* and *Alien* may keep coming back, but there are as many dissimilarities as there are similarities – either in the villains or the heroes and heroines.

Diverse villains will bring out new or unexposed weaknesses and provide opportunities for new areas of growth for your hero or heroine in every book you write with that main character. But dealing with the villain should be a question in the reader's mind as well. We know how to defeat a vampire and some of the methods of exposing the creature, but the question needs to be how will this hero or heroine learn that secret and succeed?

Finally, as you construct your villain you also need to determine the final outcome for your bad guy, gall or creature. We'll discuss that in a later chapter as well. Whatever you choose to do with your villain is a choice you will need to make an author – whether or not you want to destroy your villain or keep him/her/it around for another book.

Great Villains

Creatures -- *Alien Series, Jurassic Park/World series*
Jealous Lover – Alex, *Fatal Attraction*
Greedy Villain – Fagin, *Oliver*
Wrathful Villain -- Emperor Palpatine – *Star Wars* series
Corrupt Leader -- The Sheriff of Nottingham – *Robin Hood*

CHAPTER 5

The Role of Your Villain

*If you don't have a villain, the good guy
can stay home..*
Christopher Walt, Actor

Once you have determined what kind of villain you want in your story and started to look at the motivation of your villain, it is time to start deciding how you will begin to reveal that motivation to the reader in your particular story. The motivational component is perhaps one of the most important elements of creating a villain. You need to give your villain a believable reason for his or her nasty actions. A space creature who is out to conquer the world may simply be a different species looking for a new food source. Remember the aliens in the *Independence Day* movies? They wanted the earth's resources to save their way of life, and they were willing to kill everyone on the planet to achieve their goals. Their technology was eons ahead of man's capabilities, and it took an all-out battle before humans were able to fight them off.

Motivation could also be an internal issue, such as the villain believes the hero killed his sister and wants revenge. Or more probable, the motivation could also be some type of an external problem such as the hero is striving for the same goal as the villain, the same girl, the same job.

The more internal reasons you can give your villain, the more you will raise the conflict, especially if the villain and the hero want/desire the same goal/dream/person/reward, etc. Motivation is critical. Just as you build motivation into your main characters, you need to build it in your villains. No one is going to believe your conflict if the motivation driving your villain is not strong.

While your story should be a battle between your protagonist and the antagonist, it doesn't need to start out that way, especially when writing fantasy or science fiction. You might have a villain who sets out to take control of a village or a planet simply for greed or for a quest for power. However, the hero/heroine thwarts the villain somehow and proves to be the most capable foe so the villain focuses more attention on that person. Perhaps there is a prophecy that the hero is the person who will defeat the villain eventually so the villain sets out to destroy the hero first.

Hero against villain changes the overall story structure so the battle become personal. It becomes a battle between the hero and the bad guy. The hero's journey begins with his/her fight against the villain, even if that person doesn't know who it is. The hero simply knows that someone or something is causing a problem and sets out to solve it. The battle really narrows when the villain realizes who is coming after him/her. Then the villain's motivation may become personal and that is what you want to happen. At that point the villain wants to destroy the hero as well as all he stands for in the story.

As the story progresses, you want to increase that tension between the villain and the hero/heroine. Again, it can be a direct or physical attack or it can be something that is a psychological battle. Make every interaction count, just as you would between your main characters.

Once you have set the villain's motivation, you need to take the story to the next level. At this point, you will need to begin to establish the relationship with the protagonist. As we just noted the story doesn't necessarily need to start out as the hero against the villain, but once the two face off, it does need to become a personal battle.

Earlier we mentioned Hans Gruber in the first *Die Hard* movie, who was a true bad-ass terrorist. He was only out for money when he ran up against police officer John McClain. As we noted, McClain was not just a cop doing his duty -- he was fighting to save his wife. But on the other side, the battle also turned personal for the bad guys when McClain killed the brother of Karl, one of the terrorists. While the struggle had always been personal for McClain, now it also became a grudge match between McClain and Karl. The overall result was a movie premise that could have been just a shoot-out thriller but instead turned into two sequels.

Another type of struggle that is personal might be when a friend or former acquaintance turns on the hero. Nothing could be worse than learning that a friend is actually the enemy – such as Anakin Skywalker betraying Obie Wan Kenobi. What could be more personal than a battle between old friends?

What about a fight against a known enemy who has beaten your hero in the past? Professor Moriarty hated Sherlock Holmes for stopping all his various evil activities, and it became an individual—and personal—battle to overcome and defeat his mortal enemy.

A disagreement with a relative can also be very personal. Edmond was tormented by his illegitimate birth in *King Lear*. Luke Skywalker became a tortured soul when he discovered his father was the villain Darth Vader. How many stories have featured arguments between father and son, sister and brother or brother against brother?

What about a battle with a former lover? We've mentioned *Fatal Attraction*, where villainess Alex felt betrayed by her lover when she didn't get her way. She was not content to be simply a one-night stand. She was going to invade her lover's life and make him suffer. The people around him were going to suffer, even if they didn't know why. Many a book or movie have featured ex-lovers as villains who are out for revenge.

Jealous lovers, friends, siblings or spouses also make great villains. Anger or envy can be the catalyst that turns a friend, lover, spouse or close relative into an enemy and the hero or heroine might not suspect or realize what is happening. The hero or heroine may feel so close to that particular person that he/she can't conceive of that lover, wife/husband, brother/sister, mother/father trying to cause problems. The book and movie, *Presumed Innocent,* features a man who stands trial for murdering an ex-lover. He and a friend try to find out who did it, but their quest takes them in the wrong direction. The real killer is so close to him, he never overlooks the truth.

Presenting Your Villain

Once you have created and developed your villain, you must decide how to reveal or present the villain to the reader. Unmasking the villain in a mystery can be one of the high points of your book, movie or screenplay. In a thriller it might be done in a grand way at the beginning as the bad guy squares off with the good guys. It might also be a slow reveal where the reader/viewer begins to question the villain's motives until he/she is finally coming fully into focus as the bad guy/gal.

Revealing the villain can be done in a number of different ways, and the sky is the limit. This is the time to be very creative as you are constructing your story and your characters. How you decide to reveal the truth can also depend on the genre of story you are writing.

Will you:

Present the villain from the beginning and make the story a game of cat and mouse?

Reveal the villain early and make it a story about defeating the antagonist?

Keep the villain a secret for most of the story but let the hero or heroine figure it out and then try to stop the villain?

Keep the villain a secret until the very end and spring the truth on the hero or heroine for the final struggle?

Reveal the truth at the end of the plot, and after a struggle, let the villain escape for the next book?

As we have noted, determining how and when to reveal your villain can depend on the genre of book you are writing. For instance, if you are writing a romance, your reader might not even know there is a villain until the heroine discovers her mother-in-law-to-be or perhaps her father has been working to keep the two lovers apart.

In a mystery or suspense book or screenplay, you probably won't reveal the bad guy until the last few pages when the hero/heroine figures out the meaning of all the clues and confronts the villain.

If you are writing a thriller, you might reveal the bad guy early. The plot can then become a matching of wits, where the hero or heroine must stop the villain before that person can carry out an evil plan.

In a fantasy story, the villains might be numerous. They could be embodied in one or two leaders, but they could also be members of another tribe or nameless vampires who are trying to prey on the innocent people of a nearby kingdom or town. They could also be a hoard of zombies who are bent on taking over a whole territory as they roam the countryside. The villains might also be members of an army or evil oppressors who want to subjugate a peaceful country.

In science fiction books or movies, you might let the reader know only a little about the identity of the space invaders or who the foe is. The hero and heroine must then determine how to conquer the aliens. That was what H.G. Wells did in *War of the Worlds* and what was done in the movies, *Independence Day* or *Signs*. In those stories, the humans got to know a little about their enemies but they had no clue how to deal with them or to defeat them or even why the aliens had come to earth. They had to learn about the space visitors in order to discover what could drive them away and save mankind.

On the other hand, in the *Star Wars* movies, we learned from the beginning that the entire story was set in a different time and place. In this case, we learned that the bad guys were the forces of the evil Empire. The battle between the rebel alliance and the Empire had been going on for years in the first movie.

If you are writing a fantasy or science fiction story, that may be the course you choose to take as you select your villains. Still, though it might be a situation where there is one opposing army against another, you will want your story to become personal for the reader or audience. The plot might involve a war, but your story will probably be told from the point of view of one or two characters as they face the individual problems of the war. Even if you are writing an epic fantasy with multiple viewpoints, you should decide on who the heroes are and who the villains are and how much of their stories you want to present. That can help to make your story become more personal. You might have an entire army for your hero or heroine to battle, but if you focus on a certain hero or heroine's personal struggle, the reader will relate to the story much better.

CREATING A GREAT VILLAIN • 61

Readers and audiences reacted so well to the various stories told in *The Hunger Games* because of the focus on Katniss Everdeen's personal battles. In *Star Wars*, we knew Luke and Leia were battling the Empire, but the struggle also became the personal battle between Luke and his father, Darth Vader.

There can also be more than one villain if you have an epic tale, like *Star Wars*. Han wasn't as worried about the war with the Empire when we first met him. He was a simply a smuggler who had made an enemy of Jabba the Hutt. Jabba was paying bounty hunters to capture Han for abandoning his cargo and not paying him back. Originally, we didn't even see Jabba until the third movie, but as soon as we met him, we knew he was the enemy. When he was brought in for the re-release of *Star Wars*, we were given the backstory that discussed their earlier dealings. He had proven to be such a popular villain in that third film he was brought in from the very beginning for the new generation of audiences.

If you are writing a thriller, you might make your story a taut tale where there is a time factor and a battle between the hero/heroine and the villain. In *Silence of the Lambs*, we already knew Hannibal Lecter was a bad guy. He was in prison for murder, and while he wasn't the culprit in this story, we knew he couldn't be trusted.

The villain of that particular story was unknown, though police suspected Lecter knew who he was. As Clarice questioned Lecter and he agreed to help her, we weren't certain if he was guiding her in the right direction toward the killer or just playing with her for his own amusement. At the same time, readers and viewers *discovered* who the villain was and even saw him take another victim. The suspense built because Clarice didn't know who the man was and we didn't know where he was. The pressure of time and the unknown built into an almost unbearable tension until Clarice knocked on a door and came face to face with the villain without knowing it, but the viewers knew, and it added to their fear for her.

That is the sort of tension that can enthrall readers and begin to build an audience for an author. The readers or viewers remember the scare or the chill that ran down their spine as the villain was revealed. As readers and viewers, we had no idea if Clarice could figure things out. Or would the villain succeed in capturing her and tossing her into the well too?

How will you divulge your villain? Again, the unveiling can be done right from the beginning, or it can be kept a secret until YOU want to divulge it to the audience or readers with a big surprise as Thomas Harris did in *Silence of the Lambs*.

That brings us to another problem some mystery or suspense writers have. When does the writer determine WHO the villain is? Do you need to know the identity when you begin to write your book? Some writers who are careful plotters say they cannot begin writing their story until they know most of the details. On the other hand, seat-of-the-pants writers say they like to uncover their villains as they go along. What if you discover that you have chosen the wrong villain and want to change who it is halfway through the story?

This can be a real problem, especially for mystery, suspense or thriller writers. Common sense dictates that the writer should know the mystery villain right from the beginning so that clues can be planted along the way for readers to find. Many mystery readers enjoy looking for clues and being able to see if they are right at the end of the book.

However, while you should know the villain from the beginning, at times a villain might surprise an author and suddenly show up and change the plot. If you decide on a different villain or motive as you write the book, don't fret. That is where careful editing can help you.

As you develop your writing skills you will find out on your own which method works best for you – whether it is to be a careful planner or whether your writing is more creative when done organically by the seat of your pants.

However, if you are writing mystery or suspense, and the villain is due to be revealed at the end, you need to drop clues along the way for readers. They can be added later, during the editing process, but they should be there. The reason for this is that mystery and suspense readers often like to watch for the clues themselves. They like to match wits with the bad guys—and the author—along with the heroes and heroines and see if they can figure out the mystery for themselves.

This is another reason to give the unknown villain a presence in the story – as Harris did in *Silence of the Lambs*. Knowing the danger that lurks for the hero and heroine can make the tension more intense for the reader. It can become almost unbearable when the readers know what might await the protagonists, but the main characters have no idea what is coming. Seeing how the hero and heroine reacts to the situation also makes the reader see the character in a stronger and more heroic light.

Some writers even place the reader into the villain's point of view for long passages and that can give readers a close look at what the person might be planning. Again, if you are writing a mystery and you write by the seat of your pants, as we noted earlier, don't worry if you don't know your villain early in the book. That is what editing is for. If you keep writing until you decide the eventual villain, you can then go back and as you edit, you can look for places to insert clues or red herrings. Nothing is more satisfying to mystery readers than to be surprised by the killer/bad guy and then go back and look over the book and realize those small clues were planted all along. and they should have been able to see the solution themselves before the hero or heroine figure it out.

Hiding your Villains

Now let's tackle another issue in presenting the villain in your book. How do you place that villain into the plot itself without giving away his/her identity if you are writing a suspense or mystery story? The same may be true in a romance where bad things keep happening and the hero and heroine don't know who is trying to keep them apart. How do you place the villain in the story while keeping his/her identity a secret? Let's take a look at the different methods you can use to set the villain loose to cause trouble while still keeping him/her anonymous.

An initial problem is that we will need to bring in the villain's motivation to take the story to the next level. We need to establish the relationship with the protagonist, and more than anything, we need to HIDE the motivation in plain sight. Readers are going to feel cheated if they don't get to know the villain before the last few pages. They want to be able to match wits not only with the hero and heroine but with the writer to see if they can figure out who the villain is before the ending.

You also want to create suspense when creating a good villain. Even if the villain is the benign social climbing mother-in-law whose only goal is to break up the marriage of her successful son to a flamboyant nude dancer, we want to watch the struggle build between the hero and heroine and that villain until the end. Yes, we've covered that in previous chapters, but we're mentioning it again only because we want you to always keep tit in mind in your particular story as you craft your villain. Eventually the hero and heroine must face off with the villain and once the main characters square off against each other, the struggle should already be or become personal on some level.

While determining that struggle can raise a problem for the author, it can also enhance your plot. Let's examine a variety of ways to accomplish your goal of making the problem personal, but keeping the villain secret:

Make the villain a close or trusted character. A best friend, a valued employee, a devoted relative can make a good villain because the reader probably won't suspect them. They might appear to be helping the main characters get through whatever problem they have. If we have the villain turn out to be the lover of a person, that can make the struggle not only more personal but more intense. If someone is helping the hero or heroine that can also add suspense. In the book and movie, *The Girl on the Train*, the heroine, Rachel, who is an alcoholic, is trying to help Scott after his wife disappears. But there are so many things she can't remember and for as time we aren't certain if she might even be the killer. She gets help from her ex-husband, Tom, who eventually turns out to be not really be helping her. He has other motives for his actions…

Create a villain who is a charming, handsome, or gets involved romantically with your main character. In the movie, *The Net*, Angela Bennett has an affair with a man she meets while she is on vacation. But then a trusted friend is killed and someone steals her identity. Who would have suspected that the handsome stranger had been out to get her all along and their meeting was no accident? Often, we are rooting for that special person to become the romantic partner for the hero or heroine so we don't expect the author or screenwriter to make the person the villain.

One of the charming aspects of the movie, *Romancing the Stone*, was that we were never sure whether or not Jack Colton was going to turn out to be a villain or if he was going to end up helping Joan Wilder. We found out early in the film that one of his goals was to buy a boat to sail around the world. Once he found out about Joan's map, we knew he wanted to use it to find the stone because that would get him the money to buy his boat. We knew Joan was up against two other sets of bad guys, but the fact that yet another villain might be charming her or "romancing" her made the story even more tense. Would Jack help her in the end or would he simply take off with the map?

The villain might turn out to be someone who appears to be completely harmless or incompetent. In the movie, *The Usual Suspects,* we get the story of a heist from the viewpoint of a paralyzed character who keeps reminding us that he is "slow and crippled." But we keep hearing that the mastermind of the entire operation was the powerful Keyser Soze. The final scenes showing the discovery of Keyser's identity and what happens to him turns out to be a complete surprise. Not only that, but if you watch the movie several times, you will discover subtle hints of the truth were there all along.

On another level, there are real-life con men who are actual villains, who get away with their chicanery for years. The real-life serial killer, Ted Bundy, was not only handsome and personable, but he often conned his murder victims from the beginning. Like the killer in *Silence of the Lambs,* who used his dog to attract women, Bundy often kept a cast in his little VW. Then he could appear helpless to get his victims away from the crowd when they would try to help him. Bundy continued his cunning ways even while in jail. He went on an announced hunger strike. In the end, it turned out to be a plan to lose weight so he could slip through a narrow vent to escape—which he did.

A Mr. Nice Guy character can make a good villain. Like the friend or romantic interest of the main character or the harmless villain, this is a person who goes out of his/her way to try to help the hero or heroine or to solve a crime. He/she is trying to become the best friend even as that villain is plotting new crimes. Having the character constantly appear at a scene can be one of those elements that will have readers wondering why they didn't figure things out when he/she kept suddenly showing up. You can also use that sort of a character to pull suspicion away from the real bad guy.

An authority figure can be used as a villain or a possible villain

in a number of ways. He or she can be suspected as the villain and then turn out to be helping behind the scenes. This character might also be a respected mentor. In the *Harry Potter* series, we were never quite certain for a long time about whether or not Professor Snape was actually trying to help Harry or trying to hurt him. The final revelation of his role in Harry's life and that of Harry's parents brought the story together in a way that could never be suspected in the first story of the series.

On the other hand, as a villain, the person of authority might not be suspected as the villain because he/she appears to be trying to protect or help the hero/heroine. Instead, the authority figure is keeping the hero/heroine from learning the truth or steering him/her in the wrong direction to keep from being suspected. There are so many possibilities, and you can determine the best way to use that character as the villain. They are already in charge. They are knowledgeable. Why should they be trying to achieve more or trying to destroy the hero or heroine? The choice is yours.

The point of using these type of villains goes back to what we said earlier – wanting to have personal reasons for involving your characters with the villains. If we as readers grow to care about the main characters, their battles and struggles became personal to us. These familiar characters will become as important to the readers as they do to the heroes and heroines. We will feel just as betrayed by these unlikely villains as our heroes and heroines are when they discover who the villain is.

Memorable Villains

Charming Villain – Wickham, *Pride & Prejudice*
Harmless Villain – Ralphie, *Romancing the Stone*
Boss Villain – Bill Lumbergh, *Office Space*
Unknown Villain -- *Phantoms*

CHAPTER 6

The Hero-Villain Relationship

*"Who is to say who is the villain and who is the hero?
Probably the dictionary."*
Joss Whedan

We have been looking at creating a great villain and how that person appears in your story as he/she battles with the hero/heroine. Now let's move the process one more step forward and focus on the personal struggle that will evolve between these two special characters. We have already noted that without the villain you can't have a great hero because he or she won't have anything to do. The hero needs a villain in order to act heroic. But at the same time, the converse is also true. You cannot have a well-developed villain without a wonderful hero. You cannot fully show the villain in all his nastiness and glory until you have presented him in an all-out battle--and that should be in a personal battle--with the hero. The two of them should face off in a variety of ways that illustrate and test the best and worst characteristics of both.

How do we do that?

You've probably heard of the need for "goal, motivation and conflict" or GMC for your heroes and heroines in your books. But the same is true for your bad guys. They need their own goals, which are probably negative or going to hurt someone else. They also have their own reasons for pursuing those evil outcomes. Sometimes those reasons might simply be to cover up an evil deed. After all, their conflict can often also drive the heroine or hero's GMC, which might include a goal to destroy or at least stop the villain.

The Role of Conflict

Conflict is necessary in every story, whether it is between characters, circumstances or nature in general. It usually happens because of the INCOMPATIBILITY between two characters or forces who each have a different way or idea of how to solve a problem or deal with a situation. The villain's job is to stop, thwart or somehow deny or interfere with the goals, desires and aspirations of the hero. In other words, the villain's job is to cause conflict.

There are basically two types of conflict: that which comes from a struggle with a force outside of the character, or it might be the struggle that comes within one's self where the character must make some decision, overcome pain, quiet their temper, resist an urge, etc.

Conflict in a story does not have to be settled with lightsabers or laser guns, automatic weapons or explosions. It can be as quiet as the simple internal decisions our heroes or heroines will make on a certain issue. It can even be as deep as how far should modern science go and on which side of the question the hero or heroine might be. The mixture of science and mankind's acceptance or rejection of it can even be turned into a romantic story such as the movies *The Shape of Water* and *Avatar.* The theme of man versus science has played out in many recent science fiction books and movies with heroes against villains on both sides with conflict stemming from all different directions.

No matter where your story's conflict arises, every story must contain an element of some sort of conflict. Even the sweetest of romances or stories of faith will contain some sort of conflict. In a sweet romance it might be the heroine's choice of which hero she wants or if she is ready to let go of her own demons and marry the hero.

The villain should play a role in the overall conflict that your main character faces. If you want your main character to learn a lesson about humility, it could be that the villain teaches him or her that lesson by bringing him down a notch and the hero learns that coming out on top is not necessarily good if it requires short cuts or cheating or losing the one you love.

When things are getting bad for your protagonist, add another conflict. If your heroine solves one dilemma, put a different obstacle in front of her. If the pace slows down and the story is becoming boring, have the villain throw yet another obstacle at her—perhaps one that tests her in another way.

Even internal conflict can have rising tension. A heroine who does something dishonest can struggle with herself to rectify the situation. Obstacles thrown in her path can make it more and more difficult to redeem herself until she eventually begins to doubt herself or her worth.

This is where the villain can come in. It is because of that growing conflict that the heroine or hero must act. But then again, it might be the villain who is driving the heroine or hero to act in a bad way.

The hero/heroine then needs to figure out that the villain is pointing him/her in the wrong direction because of his/her personal desires. Overall control may be what the hero or heroine needs to realize is the problem and then he or she must overcome it in order to win the day and become the person he or she wants to be. That internal battle for the soul or heart of the hero or heroine can be every bit as difficult as a sword fight or a gun battle.

Also keep in mind that this is a personal struggle between the hero or heroine and the villain. No one else can step in and solve the problem or fix things. The protagonist can have help realizing the problem, but when it comes to solving things, the hero must either do it himself or be part of the overall solution. A cop buddy should not solve the mystery for the detective. A parent can't fight a child's battles, and the government can't suddenly step in with a program that will provide needed cash for a business. The hero/heroine must come up with the solution on his/her own. That is how the conflict works for the hero and the villain. They must face off with their varying values and traits in the course of the story, and the author should start setting up the struggle from the very beginning

How can that be accomplished?

First, you can give the hero and the villain opposing or conflicting goals right from the beginning. As we've pointed out in stories from *Titanic* to *Die Hard,* the heroine and hero in those stories had opposing goals with the villains. We've looked at the conflicts in *Die Hard*. In *Titanic*, Jack and Rose wanted to be together while Cal wanted Rose. Mostly Rose didn't want the life Cal had in mind for her. She didn't relish the idea of the idle life of a debutante whose future was filled with afternoons of meaningless chit chat or fancy dinners. She was intrigued by the idea of being free to do anything she wanted. She wanted the sort of life Jack represented and after she survived the sinking of the Titanic, she followed through on her final promise to Jack to "never let go." She went after the life Jack wanted for her as the pictures of her past that line her bed illustrated in the closing shots.

In most stories, such as *Star Wars,* the hero or heroine is going to win the day and get what he or she wants, while the villain is vanquished. Luke Skywalker and his friends are able to destroy the Death Star in *Star Wars, A New Hope,* so the threat of the Empire is pushed aside for the moment. The war may not be won, but the story of this particular battle was successful.

In the second installment, Darth Vader and the Empire are back as villains, but Luke is growing stronger and he starts his training to become a Jedi. But there are new villains too. Besides space monsters, Han and Leia are betrayed by an old friend and Han is taken by bounty hunters.

As the story closes, Luke makes a horrendous discovery: the villain he is fighting is actually his father. Now he is truly conflicted. Luke makes the decision not to give in to the Dark Side as this story ends, but the battle with his father is not over. The ending of this movie actually set up the next installment between hero and villain.

The movie goers knew that Luke would need to face his father again. This sort of conflict is what you want to create between your heroes, heroines and the villains. They usually have individual, differing goals, or opposite goals.

In some cases, the hero and villain may want the same thing. In many romances, the battle between the villain and the hero/heroine is simple—each wants a certain person. In *Titanic,* Cal wanted Rose; so did Jack. In other cases, it could be the leadership of a town council or as big as a world, or the universe, as was the case in the Star Wars movies. The difference might be that each would rule it in different ways. For instance, in the *Star Wars* series, the Empire believed in running roughshod over other worlds and taking total control, while those in opposition would leave worlds free while the Jedi patrolled the universe using the power of the Force.

Both want the same thing – they just have different ideas and methods for how they will achieve their goal.

This is where conflict really comes into the picture. There is usually a big difference in how the hero or the villain view achieving their goal. While the hero or heroine might be ready to work for their happy ending, the villain has no constraints on him or her.

With the villain, it is all or nothing, and they do not see losing as an option. They want to win at all costs, no matter who they hurt or what happens to anyone around them. Winning and getting their way is the only option they see and they are willing to do anything to get it. This is what makes them villains. They are willing to shed any constraints, risk anything or anyone to get their desired outcome.

For the writer, the more ruthless the villain becomes, the stronger they will be and thus they also become greater foes for the hero and the heroine. Defeating a strong villain will create a stronger hero/heroine and their overall conflict frames the relationship.

Let's look deeper into how you can create more of the conflict in your book between the hero and the villain and how you can use that to help your hero.

As we noted earlier, the hero has to solve his/her problems in order to achieve the happy ending. But it is also because of the particular challenges that the villain poses that makes that hero or heroine grow and become stronger as a person. There are a number of ways to accomplish or illustrate this for your readers:

Give the heroes and villains opposing goals – in other words, one wants black to win, one wants white to win. This is the battle between the villain and hero that we see so often. In the *Star Wars* movies, as we discussed, Darth Vader wants the Empire to rule the universe while Luke Skywalker and his friends want to get rid of the Empire and return to the days when the Jedi knights kept peace throughout the galaxy.

This method is used most often in books and movies. The hero wants the "good" side to win, while the dark-hearted villain will go to any lengths to have his own side come out victorious, and that opposing side is usually going to hurt someone.

Give heroes and villains the *same* goal but they try to achieve it in opposing ways – In the movie, *Titanic*, both Jack and Cal want to see Rose survive. They both love her and want to see that she is safe. While both are willing to do anything to accomplish that, Cal is also willing to use any underhanded trick he can to keep her from surviving with Jack. He first frames Jack for stealing the jewel, and then when Jack escapes, he has his henchman try to kill Jack.

In your books, again, this is good versus bad where the good will look for more virtuous ways of winning, while the villain will try any underhanded method possible to come out on top. Make the heroes and villains friends with the same goal at the beginning and then turn the sides against each other.

Make the heroes and villains bitter enemies from childhood.
Just as the hero and villain can have started as friends it may be that the villain was the hero's nemesis from an early age. Do we ever get over those who bested us when we were young?

From the time he was a young man, George Bailey in *It's a Wonderful Life* had seen his family's savings and loan company doing battle with Mr. Potter's bank across town. At one point he gave up the money for his wedding trip to stay home and save the day but still Mr. Potter continued to put pressure on his family and on their savings and loan company. When his uncle makes a mistake with a deposit, Mr. Potter sees a way to finally throw George in jail and fully control the town. But George discovers he has been a true hero to the people of Bedford Falls. They join together to keep him out of jail on Christmas Eve, showing him that he really has lived a wonderful life.

Presenting Your Villain

Once you have brought your villain onto the written page, you must also decide how he/she is going to be seen and heard by the reader. Will your villain be known before the end of the story or will he/she be simply a character floating around in the background committing evil deeds until the final unveiling? We have looked at methods to bring villains into your story so that they are not complete strangers to the reader when the truth finally comes out. Now let's look at some different ways to bring them and their *thoughts* into the story. A good way to ratchet up the tension in a thriller or mystery is to give readers just enough information so that they have a vague idea of what might be coming. But perhaps readers don't know for certain when or where the bad event will happen. They might also not be certain about why the villain wants to strike. Unknown factors can keep the reader or movie-goer on edge as the villains plan or carry out a destructive plan. The audience in *Die Hard* knew John McClane was up against a large number of heavily-armed terrorists, but he had no clue when he started out.

At the same time, the villains didn't realize he was a police officer with special skills. In *Die Hard II*, neither the audience nor McClane knew that the commandos who were supposed to help him were actually traitors who were part of the traitorous group. The audience discovered their treachery when he learned of it. That brings us to Point of View or POV. *WHO* is telling your story? What the audience knows or learns depends on who that point-of-view person is. Is the POV totally in the hands of your hero or heroine? Do we sometimes get the story from the villain's perspective? Also, is the

POV in first person or third person? Point of View can make a big difference in how you construct your story and how it comes across to the reader or viewer. There are a number of ways to write Point of View:

First Person means that everything is told from one person's viewpoint. *I am* directly telling the story and the reader is only going to get *my* observations. But it goes beyond that. You as the author get to decide if *I* will tell the story directly, or if the story will also be told through other character's eyes, in Third Person (*he* or *she*). If you write the entire book in First Person the reader will get only one person's point of view. The First-Person viewpoint is often used in mystery or Young Adult books, but it can also be used to good advantage in science fiction, horror or romantic comedy.

Second Person is rarely used so we won't be discussing it here.

Again, as a refresher, in second person the author refers to "you" as one of the characters, taking the reader into the story as though he/she is relating it directly to you.

Third Person is the most frequently used Point of View. In that case, the author refers to everyone as "he," "she," or "it." Of course, if you use Third Person you can tell the story from several POVs so it offers the most flexibility in your writing. You can also use a combination of First and Third and that can be very helpful and intriguing when writing villains. You can use different POVs in several ways.

Write the hero or heroine's story in Third Person, but put the villain's Point of View in First Person. The advantage is that readers know the villain's thoughts and what the villain is planning. Readers are placed directly in the villain's thoughts so they also know why the villain is acting the way he/she is and his/her feelings about the hero and heroine. This method can make the villain more sympathetic or appear more nasty if the reader realizes there is NOTHING this killer or criminal won't do to get his or her own way.

Write everyone in third person. In this scenario, you can tell what is in the villain's head but it isn't quite as direct as first person. The reader is going to know what is being planned by the villain, though again, YOU get to choose how much they tell and how much information you want to give the reader ahead of time. If the villain is plotting a killing or to plant a bomb, you can keep part of the plan a mystery to increase the tension.

Write the hero or heroine in first person and put the villain in third person. Again, you can let the reader know some of what is in the villain's head, but you also put the reader directly in the main character's head. This can make the reader relate more to the main character, and it brings in suspense if the reader knows something is being planned but the hero doesn't know.

Rival Villains

Mr. Potter – *It's a Wonderful Life*
Ace Merrill – *Stand by Me*
Katharine – *Working Girl*
The Joker – *Batman*
Lex Luther – *Superman*

CHAPTER 7

The Villain's Arc

*Villains are meant to be black hearted in
popular novels. If you say I have a good-hearted villain,
then I've failed.*
Ken Follett

Now that we have looked at creating our villains and putting them into the story, let's take a closer look at the villain's progression in the story from beginning to end. In other words, we're going to explore the emotional **character arc** of our story villains.

What is an ARC?

A character arc is a word picture of the emotional status of the character as he or she moves through the storyline or through a series of scenes. Characters begin the story with a certain viewpoint and through the events in the story, that viewpoint may begin to change for some of them. The various situations that the characters encounter during the story can shift the course of their lives or affect their viewpoint or outlook on life and change the lives of those around them as well going forward. Like any person who continues to grow throughout life, a character may change because of the events in the story. In fact, we recommend it. Your main characters should be growing and changing at least a little during any story. In a series novel, it might be a small change for the main character, but it will happen. Think of how Harry Potter and his friends continued to grow over the course of that series. Even in a long-running detective series, the detective will grow and change somewhat in each story, or at least he/she will learn something. The character of Kinsey Milhone who started in the first *A is for Alibi* book was a little different by the time the series reached *Y is for Yesterday*. The character of Harry Bosch continues to develop and change in Michael Connelly's story of a rugged police officer in Los Angeles.

In the case of the hero or heroine, the change in the character in each individual story will probably be for the better. The hero or heroine may learn a life lesson or discover strengths he or she didn't know he had. The character may make a decision that will benefit his/her life in the future or uncover talents he or she didn't know he/she had.

The character arc or character growth is usually different for the villain. If the villain is directly at odds with the hero or heroine, the end result will be that the hero/heroine wins and the villain is vanquished, killed, goes to jail or disappears.

The story of discovery that we described for the hero/heroine may also occur for the villain, though it will be illustrated in a different way. Unless you are dealing with a redeemable or minor villain, the character journey will only get worse for your villain. In many cases the villain will make a life or death decision at the end of the story. He or she won't want to live on in the new circumstances that are about to change or he/she will be locked up or put away forever. It could also be that his or her death will be required in order for the hero and heroine to get the peace each deserves or has won. In some cases, the villain may be allowed to escape, especially if you are planning on writing a series and using the villain in numerous stories, or the villain might be redeemed or realize the error of his or her ways.

Whatever you decide to do with your villain, the story will follow a certain path or story arc that allows your villain to show himself or herself from the beginning until the ending. Just like the hero/heroine is following a certain journey or arc, the villain will also be part of that arc but in the opposite way. The difference is that you will be conducting most of the events that happen to the hero and heroine in the storytelling itself. On the other hand, the villain's story will be occurring in the background, but you may not be showing it to readers on the written page. They will see only what YOU want them to see and will learn only what you want them to know. If you plan to keep your villain's identity secret, much of his/her story *must* occur in the background. You don't want to risk the reader discovering the truth until YOU divulge it.

Let's look at how the story arc proceeds in most stories:

An ARC first sets up the action or plot points of the overall story. Then the arc traces the characters' internal emotional, psychological and personal change the character undergoes throughout the story.

Just like the main characters or protagonists, the villain must wrestle with the problems, catastrophes, accidents and concerns that take place in the story. Often the villain is the cause of those catastrophes or problems. Over the course of the story, the hero or heroine must solve the problems and while his/her story arc begins to go lower as things get worse, in the case of the villain, his or her story arc will rise as he/she succeeds in causing problem after problem. His or her high point should be the hero/heroine's low point. Then as the hero and heroine's arc rises, the villain's arc begins to fall. Eventually, he/she will be taken down by either being exposed, killed, jailed, thrown out or in some cases, forgiven by the end of the story or book.

If you are writing a series, the villain might escape to fight another day. As we've said before, though, if you are going to do that, you must solve some sort of other issue for your main characters. For instance, in first episode of *Star Wars*, back in the 1970s, the rebels saved their base from destruction and they were able to get rid of the original Death Star. However, the evil villain Darth Vader escaped, and while we heard about the Emperor, we never met him, though we knew he was lurking in the background.

As we have noted on several occasions, just like your leading characters, any great villain has a goal in mind when the story starts. It is often this goal that actually sets up the beginning of the story itself. Your main characters may simply want to live a normal life or get ahead in the world, but the villain is already hard at work, and that will drastically change life for your hero or heroine.

For instance:

In *Star Wars*, the story starts with the Princess trying to escape with the plans for the Death Star. The Empire has built the Death Star, but the rebels don't know it is functional. They just want to get their hands on the plans so they can find a way to destroy it.

When Darth Vader captures her transport, she jettisons the robots with the plans, trying to get them to Obi Wan Kenobi so he can get them safely to the rebel leaders. The battle lines are set between the forces of good and evil – the rebel forces want to destroy the Death Star before it begins destroying all their planets. On the other side, the Empire wants to start destroying the rebel bases with the Death Star. Both arcs – for the heroes and the villains – are starting to take off.

The story arc for the two opposing sides actually looks like an eye if you think about it. Both the villains and hero/heroine start from the same position in the middle. The fortunes of the villain begin rising from the first action, while those of the heroes begin to get lower as they have to battle back against increasingly bad events. The lowest point for the heroes is the highest point for the villain. Then as the hero fights back, the villain's fortunes start to fall until they converge at the end.

One thing you need to keep in mind as you write your story: **It is the action of the villain that sets the storyline in motion.** The hero could go on living a normal or quiet life if the villain didn't come into his/her world and kill or kidnap someone, release the evil creature or virus or sow the seeds of discord in a growing romance.

Let's look at another story: In *Romancing the Stone*, Joan Wilder wants to continue living her life as a romance novelist, even if it is on the drab side. She would like to find a romantic hero of her own, but she doubts it will happen. Then along comes Colonel Zolo. He is the Minister of Antiquities in his Latin American country, but he has been stealing treasures from the government for years and he has been killing people when he needs to—like Joan Wilder's brother-in-law who had a map of the whereabouts of a fabulous gem.

He might also have killed Joan's sister, if she hadn't already been kidnapped by Ira and Ralph, who also want that map. The three villains – the colonel, Ira and Ralph – all have the possession of that stone as their goal, but Joan has the map to the gem's location and stands in their way. It is their desire to obtain the map which sets everything in motion.

For the colonel and her sister's kidnappers, the plot action begins to rise when they realize Joan has the map and all they need is to get it from her. For Joan, her fortunes begin to sink when she gets the map because she must go to Colombia and turn it over to her sister's kidnappers. The action has started for everyone, but it is going in different directions. Joan's arc is sinking because her life has been disrupted, but the arc is rising for the others because they know who has the map – they just need to get it.

In *Star Wars*, Luke's fortunes begin to sink when he and his uncle buy the robots, though he doesn't know it. He doesn't even realize it when he cleans out the memory of the robots and sees part of the message from the princess. He is simply frustrated because he wants to become a pilot but he sees no way he will ever leave his uncle's farm. He certainly doesn't have time to help the princess or deliver the secret plans the robot carries. But then the robots take off and lead Luke to Obi Wan Kenobi who tells him about his Jedi father. When his aunt and uncle are killed by the Empire's forces seeking the robots, he loses his current life, and his goals shift. He is ready to join forces with Obi Wan to get the secret plans to the rebels. His story arc now has started.

In both of those cases, it is the villains' goals that really set the story arcs in motion.

In the case of your story, it could be:

A **cozy mystery** where a villain wants a piece of jewelry from her aunt's collection that she feels went to the wrong person – the heroine. The villain is willing to steal it to get it, and makes an attempt, but ends up killing the heroine's friend. The villain sets the arc in motion by trying to steal the gem and killing the friend. The heroine's arc begins to go lower because she has lost her friend. Now the villain has two goals – keep the heroine from finding who killed her friend and get the gem. The villain's arc is rising in action as she makes attempts to get the gem, while the heroine's arc is going lower as she tries to discover who killed her friend and why someone is breaking into her apartment or nearly running her off the road. Only by uncovering the truth will the heroine's fortunes rise. When she discovers who the villain is, or in one final standoff where she defeats the villain, will her fortunes rise while the villain goes to jail.

A **romance** about a female villain wanting to cause problems with a rival so she can win the man of her dreams, and she is willing to go to almost any underhanded lengths to get her way. The villain's fortunes rise as she causes nasty little problems or comes between the heroine and the hero. The heroine's arc goes lower as she struggles to win the hero's love. Only when he chooses the heroine does her character arc rise while the villain's falls.

A **medical thriller** where the evil boss is willing to work his employees to near death to develop an illegal drug so that he can make a big profit and sell the company. The hero and heroine begin to suspect what he is up to when the drug kills several people. The villain's fortunes are rising as the money rolls in, but their arc goes lower as they lose friends or see them destroyed. When the hero and heroine expose the villain, their arc goes up and his sinks when he is arrested.

A **science fiction** book where aliens plot to take over the world and only the hero and heroine realize they are starting to walk among the regular population. The villains' fortunes rise as more aliens arrive on earth, but the hero and heroine's arcs fall as humankind grows smaller. Only when the hero and heroine figure out how to destroy the aliens will their arc rise while the villains' arc falls. In the end the villains must either leave Earth or be destroyed while the hero and heroine get their world back but with new appreciation for it.

A **fantasy time travel** where the heroine ends up trapped in the past and can't find her way back to the regular world while the villain plots to use her to get to the future to change the past. Again, the fortune of the heroine and her success are directly tied to stopping the villain's plan.

If the villain's goals are in direct contrast to the protagonist, the conflict between the two starts out stronger and will move the story along at a better pace. That was the case in *Romancing the Stone* where Joan was constantly up against Colonel Solo and Ralphie. Solo first tries to steal her map and then directs her to the wrong bus. From then on it becomes a chase with her on the run and him following her.

But you can also choose to write your story so that the villain starts out with instant success in his or her evil plan but the story revolves around the hero or heroine fighting back. Then it results in a one-on-one struggle as in *Die Hard.* That conflict started with the crooks taking over the building to steal the certificates. It became a personal battle when John McClane fought back and began to kill the terrorists.

This is often the case when you are dealing with a larger than life villain and an "everyday" hero or a case when writing fantasy or science fiction. You might have a villain who sets out to take control of a village or a planet simply for greed or as a quest for power. However, the hero/heroine thwarts him somehow. Perhaps there is even a prophecy that this person will thwart him. That makes the battle become personal. The villain's motivation becomes as personal as that of the main character. This can make for an even better story.

On the other hand, even if the villain has an impersonal goal, the hero or heroine needs a personal reason to fight the bad guy, whether it is saving a family member or loved one, all of mankind, or a certain way of life. Eventually the struggle will come down to the battle between the villain and the hero in the story, whether it is just one person, a whole village or army being led by the hero or heroine.

In the case of creatures who are villains – like *Alien,* or the space invaders in *Independence Day,* or S*igns,* or the dinosaurs in *Jurassic Park* – there may no direct link to particular heroes and heroines. In these cases, the story becomes personal because we meet particular people who are affected by the creatures' actions or who help defeat the creatures. We see personal stories of courage or defiance. We must become invested in a personal way in the struggle or we are not going to be interested. In the movie, *Signs,* people were battling all around the world against alien creatures, but we only saw one tortured farm family's struggle to survive a scary night. But they also needed to face down their personal issues and overcome them and that struggle was what helped the family defeat the creatures who challenged them.

In the movie, *Alien,* the battle eventually comes down to a one- on-one battle between Ripley and the Alien. Both are fighting for survival. Only one can win. The alien needs the space ship to go to another world as much as Ripley needs to go home aboard it. In the *Jurassic Park* movies, the dinosaurs simply want to survive, but then so do the people, so it becomes a struggle for survival for both. But as much as we want to see the magnificent creatures live, there are children involved, so we need to see them saved.

In story/movie like *Signs* or *Independence Day,* the ending is not a complete victory, though the heroes and humans survive. The villains may be vanquished for now and the humans win, but the villains are not completely eliminated. The threat is gone, but it could come back. But that is a story for another day, and that can be a useful tool for bringing your readers back again. Create a strong enough villain – like Hannibal Lector, the Alien or scary dinosaurs – and readers or movie goers will be clamoring for their return.

With that in mind, let's delve deeper into the villain's story.

Creating the Villain's Arc

While a protagonist's arc goes from a tackling a problem through a series of incidents aimed at helping to make our heroes and heroines grow stronger until they change and reach a satisfactory resolution, the villain's arc is just the opposite. The villain is the force who creates the initial problem that sets the story in motion. The villain's arc begins to rise with the initial victory of the opposing force. It shows the villain's path of destruction as he, she or it, sets story events in motion, battles the protagonist and attempts to overcome all obstacles in order to be victorious. In other words, the problem that starts the story usually begins or develops as a result of the villain's goals.

Depending on your story, there are several elements to a villain's arc, and each one can result in reactionary plot points in your overall story. It is important to remember that the villain's plot points should constantly increase the tension in the protagonist's life, while the hero's reaction will increase the tension in the villain's life or perhaps spur him/her on to even worse deeds.

If you look at the villain's arc in comparison to the hero's, they should basically be opposite from the beginning of the story. As the action rises and the villain's fortune goes higher, the life and emotional concerns of the main character or hero/heroine begin to get lower. When the main character succeeds, the fortune of the villain goes down.

Let's look at some simple basics in the story arc. It might begin with a straight line for the villain and another for the main character. The lines may be equal at the beginning of the story, but in a villain's arc, their story begins to rise from the first pages as they set their evil plans in motion or begin causing problems for the hero or heroine.

Thus, our main characters' arc, or storyline, begins to descend as their happy life runs into problems. The action continues to accelerate as the villain's fortunes rise and the hero/heroine's fortunes continue to go down. We've gone through this with several characters in different movies, now let's try it with a generic villain to show you how to do it yourself:

The villain kills a person, or sets off a bomb, or arrives on the scene and the good/normal days for the hero or heroine are at an end. Let's start out looking at the way a storyline goes in a linear fashion.

>	Introduction to the regular world – a straight line for both

>	Villain sets action in motion with Inciting Incident -- Villain's arc begins rising

>	Hero/Heroine caught off guard – character arc begins to decline

>	Reaction from Hero/Heroine slows the rise of the Villain's arc

>	Villain does something worse – Villain's arc (and tension) rises; H/H arc goes lower

>	Hero/Heroine react/thwart Villain – again slow the rise in the villain's arc

>	Villain's does something worse in reaction

>	H/H arc goes lower while villain's climbs higher

> Hero/Heroine try to regroup – unsuccessfully -- arc dips lower
>
> Villain's arc rising and prepares for final triumph
>
> Hero/Heroine arc near bottom – Black Moment – change/growth in order
>
> Final Struggle -- Climax
>
> Villain is defeated – his arc drops
>
> Hero/Heroine victorious – their arc rising
>
> Final Resolution – Hero/Heroine in new world

Let's see how this plays out using a movie that should be very familiar to all, *The Wizard of Oz*. We will use the example of Miss Gulch/The Wicked Witch as our villain.

Here's the beginning of a timeline for the story's villain as she battles our heroine, Dorothy.

> Introduction of Dorothy's world on the farm which seems so ordinary
>
> Miss Gulch claims Dorothy's dog Toto bit her and takes Toto away (Inciting Incident) Her arc begins to rise while Dorothy's begins to sink below normal
>
> Dorothy runs away from home to get Toto and a tornado carries them to a new land. – her arc is continuing in a downward fashion
>
> The Wicked Witch appears and discovers Dorothy's falling house killed her sister – her rising arc is thwarted momentarily

She vows to get even with Dorothy so her arc begins to rise again

Main Character's Reaction – Dorothy gets the ruby slippers and decides to go to the Emerald City to get Wizard's help in getting home – her fortunes are going lower because she faces a trip through the unknown land

Wicked Witch attacks Dorothy along the way – villain's arc is rising while Dorothy's continues to sink

Dorothy meets Scarecrow, Tin Man and Lion who agree to help her as her arc continues to descend from Wicked Witch's surprise attacks

Wicked Witch grows stronger using poppy fields to delay Dorothy and her friends; Witches arc still rising

Dorothy's arc goes lower as they arrive at Emerald City and Witch threatens city; Wizard refuses help unless they destroy the Witch

Wicked Witch captures Dorothy at her Castle; Witch is on the verge of total victory – top of her arc – Dorothy is at lowest point on hers

Dorothy tosses water on the witch and destroys her – villain is vanquished – bottom of Villain arc – Dorothy's goes higher

Dorothy and friends return with broom only to discover Wizard is a fraud – arc is stalled

Black moment for Dorothy – another drop in her arc – she can't get home

Good Witch appears to ask what Dorothy has learned

> Dorothy has changed – learned the value of home – her arc begins to rise
>
> Final Resolution – Dorothy goes home – top of her arc

Remember, without the villain acting from the very beginning, there would be no story. If there was no Miss Gulch/witch character, Dorothy wouldn't have run away from home to save Toto. She would have been home when the family took refuge in the storm cellar. She wouldn't have been left on her own during the tornado and she wouldn't have been whisked into the sky by the storm.

The same is true once she arrives in Oz. She might have made the trip to see the Wizard because she wanted to go home, but the journey would have been much simpler if she didn't have the Witch following her and trying to stop her along the way with firebombs and poisoned poppies.

Once she reached Oz, the meeting with the Wizard might have gone differently if the Witch hadn't threatened the Emerald City because of Dorothy. Again, it becomes a personal battle between Dorothy and the Witch. Now Dorothy must destroy her and get her broom before the Wizard will grant Dorothy's wish to send her home. Her goal of getting home continually revolves around the battle with the Witch, who is out for revenge because Dorothy killed her sister.

This story line shows why the villain's arc is needed:

> To keep the tension high with external battles and reactions
>
> To keep the conflict going and cause more internal and external conflicts

The arc shows how more actions and reactions by the villain result in corresponding reactions by the main character. Those external reactions also result in more internal or emotional reactions by the villain. As the action rises, the pace of the plot picks up and moves quicker too. At the same time, the tension is increasing as the fortunes of our hero and heroine get lower as a result of the reactions of the villain.

As the battle gets more intense between the good forces and the evil, the strength of both sides is being tested. By the time they all face the final struggle, the sides should be even or the evil side may even appear to have the advantage. The reader should want the good forces to win, but their eventual triumph should be in doubt until the end. Can they break through and win the day? What will it take for them to conquer the evil forces? Could the evil side be stronger?

It is at this point that the good forces need to make their final attempt at growth, change, or discovery that leads to their winning the day. It is this final struggle that brings about the breakthrough that teaches the main character how strong he or she is. All along the way in the magical land of Oz, Dorothy is seeing that her drab life in Kansas might be much better than she realized. In Kansas, she has people who care about her, and life is less hazardous than in a land where witches cast spells, flying monkeys can carry off people, and wizards can pretend to be great heroes. She makes the final realization that she doesn't need to go looking for a better place to live. She wants to be at home among the people who love her.

As you reach the climax of your story, both your main characters and your villain will reach their breaking point. It is at this point where your main character or heroine/hero will need to either grow or make the final discovery of how to defeat the villain and the fortunes of the villain will begin to diminish.

The arc helps the writer pinpoint events that will cause and/or determine the change or denouement of the villain. Using the arc, the writer can more easily add in the small conflicts and transitions as the character evolves from one state of mind to another in a slow and even pace until s/he is compelled to make a life-changing decision that will result in the character's growth and the villain's demise.

Keep in mind that the villain's arc will almost always be in direct opposition to the protagonist's character arc. A win for the hero/heroine is usually a defeat for the villain. On the other hand, every time the main characters suffer a setback or their fortunes slide downhill, the fortunes of the villain will rise. What's bad for the protagonist is good for the villain and vice versa.

Often the Inciting Incident in a story is caused by the villain, especially in suspense, science fiction and fantasy.

In a romance, the hero meeting the heroine might be the Inciting Incident, but the villain's arc still plays a major role. As we've mentioned before, it is the villain's actions keeping them apart.

For instance, in *Pride and Prejudice*, the Inciting Incident is the arrival of the Bingley family. Elizabeth doesn't like Mr. Darcy from the first time she meets him at a ball. He knows immediately she and her family are beneath him and his station. But they are still attracted to each other as they exchange barbs. When the seemingly charming Mr. Wickham comes into the picture with his dislike for Darcy and begins telling Lizzie his falsehoods, they are totally driven apart. Only as she discovers the truth about Mr. Darcy does Lizzie begin to realize what a good and giving man he is.

In most stories, as the action moves along, the hero and heroine will keep having more problems until circumstances become so horrible, they must change and face that final struggle with the villain. In the case of Joan Wilder, she had to go from timid romance writer to fearless adversary as she faced the kidnappers in a life or death struggle to rescue her sister.

In the villain's case, at times he or she will have been somewhat successful, even if some plans have gone awry or been thwarted. But for the most part, circumstances will have been improving as his or her unscrupulous doings keep the hero or heroine on the go. The villain's biggest evil plan may still be in the planning stages—like total control of the world, or a successful escape, making the big heist, or escaping justice for the murder.

Let's go back and look at Dorothy in *The Wizard of Oz* again. When she is taken captive at the witch's castle, she has hit rock bottom. She will never get home – in fact, she faces certain death. Never during the entire journey has she realized so much that all she wants to do is to be back home in normal, everyday Kansas, surrounded by her family and friends.

For the Wicked Witch, victory is nearly at hand. She is at the top of her arc. She is about to grasp her final victory and get rid of that pesky Dorothy, avenge her sister and get the ruby slippers that will give her untold power.

But then the Tin Man, the Scarecrow and the Lion show up and Dorothy has her final showdown with the Witch. Their arcs intersect as the Witch tries to destroy her friends with a burning broom to burn the Scarecrow. Dorothy's natural reaction is to try to save him. As she douses him and the Witch with water, we learn the Witch's weakness as she begins to melt. But while the Witch's arc is finished and she is destroyed, Dorothy's heroic arc will not be realized until she voices what she has learned – that there is no place like home. Only then does she go back to Kansas and her family.

The Arc is now complete. The heroine or hero is victorious while the villain faces defeat. But the main character has also learned a valuable lesson and his/her life has changed in a good way as a result.

In the case of Luke and Darth Vader, the rebels win when Luke accepts and uses the Force to fire his weapons and destroy the Death

Star, while Darth Vader, the villain, goes spinning off into space to fight another day. These two adversaries may meet again, but next time Luke will be smarter and ready to use the Force.

In the case of Joan Wilder, she has learned she is stronger than she realized. For Dorothy, it is the lesson of "there's no place like home," while for Lizzie and Mr. Darcy, it is that love can overcome pride and prejudice.

With the villain beaten in the end, the arcs are concluded and the hero/heroine are ready for a happy conclusion, while the villain suffers the final loss of the story.

Villains & Arcs

Colonel Zolo – *Romancing the Stone*
Warden Samuel Norton – *The Shawshank Redemption*
Annie Wilkes – *Misery*
Phantom – *The Phantom of the Opera*
Henry Hill – *Goodfellas*

CHAPTER 8

The Villain's Resolution

No villain thinks of himself as the villain.
John Lithgow

We have finally come to the conclusion of the villain's story. Their part of your book is finished. However, we need to look back at some of the choices you should make about your villain *before* you ever begin writing your story.

For instance, you need to consider how you will use your villain in the plot itself or if you will use the villain's viewpoint in the story. That can make a difference in how you write the book. Writing in the villain's viewpoint can make his/her motives much more direct and can even make him/her a more sympathetic character in some cases.

Letting the reader know upfront what might be in store can also heighten the tension because the reader knows what is coming, but the hero and heroine don't. That allows the reader to worry about how the good guys will handle the situation or whether they can figure things out before the evil event occurs. The anticipation can add to the reader's anxiety. How will the hero and heroine handle the tricky situation? Can they overcome the problem or will the villain win?

Putting the reader into the villain's head also lets the reader know the villain's motives and why the villain might want to carry out their evil deeds or why they might hate the hero and heroine. Again, this might make the villain more sympathetic if the reader understands the villain feeling cheated. The villain becomes more human if his/her choices seem sad and personal.

On the other hand, knowing that the villain just wants to cause pain can turn the reader against the villain. Selfish choices by the villain can also make the person even more despicable to the reader. The character of Clyde Shelton played by Gerard Butler in the movie *Law Abiding Citizen* started out as a sympathetic figure since he had lost his family. Viewers could understand why he might target the killers who got off, but taking his murderous revenge to the next level turned him from victim to villain.

This brings up another issue – how do you want the villain to be presented from the beginning of the story? Will you use his/her viewpoint? Will you let the secondary characters know who the villain is?

Let's look at some of the choices and possibilities you might want to consider when you determine what you want to do with your villain and how you want the villain to be presented from the beginning of the story.

Pros and Cons of letting the reader know villain's identity:

Pros

> The reader will delight in watching the villain plan and carry out his evil deeds

The reader can see why the villain might hate the hero.
Suspense heightened as reader knowing what is coming
The reader will better understand the villain

The villain will seem more despicable if his or her motives are selfish

The villain will appear more human if motives are real and personal

Cons

Readers may prefer to figure out the mystery for themselves

Knowing what is coming may lessen the suspense

Knowing the villain's motives might make him/her more sympathetic and less of a villain

There are plenty of reasons for keeping the villains' identities hidden until the end. Many mystery readers take great pride in acting as sleuths themselves. They prefer being able to follow the clues along with the hero/heroine to figure out who the villain is before the author reveals it. They not only want the pleasure of reading the book, but they want to pursue and watch for any tips or clues the authors might provide for them along the way. To them, a mystery might be like a treasure hunt or like following a trail of bread crumbs and getting to the right end.

Pros and cons of keeping the villain's identity secret:

Pros

Keeps the reader guessing

Allows the reader to follow the clues

Builds suspense over what happens next

Pleases the reader who figures out the right answer

Cons

Reader might feel disappointed at villain

Reader might feel cheated if not enough clues

Reader might feel misled by some of the clues

Let's take a closer look at some of these pros and cons and how to get around them to keep your story moving.

The best part of knowing who the villain is and what he/she may want to do is that it allows the reader to anticipate the hero or heroine. Think of how suspenseful a story can be if you know that villain is waiting down the street behind a building with a gun in his hand. The hero doesn't know that. How will the hero get out of that situation? We know the hero probably won't be killed, but what about his girlfriend riding in the car with him? What about that innocent bystander walking down the street? All of these things add tension to your book and can help in the pacing.

If your characters also know who the villain is, they can better prepare or fight the villain. Think of the creature in *Alien*. The people on the spaceship knew generally what they were fighting—an alien entity, but they didn't quite know the extent of how lethal it could be. Along the way, as they battled the creature, they made new discoveries that made things worse, like that it kept growing or that it bled acid and could possibly burn a hole right through the hull of their spaceship. All of their encounters heightened the tension because the viewer or reader was learning these things as the characters discovered them. In some cases, the discovery came as a result of the death of a character. The suspense grew every time crew members saw evidence of the Alien in their immediate vicinity.

On the other hand, consider a romance where the father is trying to keep his daughter away from the hero. She and the reader may know about his opposition and she might even know some of the evil deeds he is doing. How will she react to them? Will she warn the hero that her dad is the person who is secretly buying up his land and trying to get him to leave the area? Or maybe she doesn't tell the hero the first time something underhanded happens and there is a terrible result, like an accident involving another friend, who might be injured or wounded. That may make her have second thoughts. Perhaps she will grow stronger so that eventually she is finally able to realize things will not improve. They can only get worse if she doesn't take a stand. She finally sides with the hero against her father. Now her father faces a choice – will he continue to play villain and lose her? Or will he regret the accident he caused and help that friend recover or make reparations? Perhaps he might even deed the land he illegally purchased to his daughter and her new husband. In this case, she was right to challenge her father, because he is not a totally evil villain. He is simply a person who feared losing his family. Now she and her children will bring him a new generation.

Keeping Your Villain UNKNOWN

What if your characters don't know who or what they are fighting? Again, as the writer, you can use that lack of knowledge about the villain to heighten suspense. Letting the reader know that the culprit/bad guy might be anyone around the hero/heroine gives the story more tension and makes the plot more involving. The reader might want to deduce along with the protagonist on who might be causing all the trouble.

If you intend to keep your villain's identity a secret, you might want to foreshadow the person's identity in some way so that the reader doesn't feel cheated later. Especially in a good mystery you will want the reader at the end to be able to go back and say: "Why didn't I see that or figure that out?"

Also, your character might be able to figure out WHAT they're fighting without revealing WHO. If you are writing paranormal or fantasy, perhaps you might want the protagonist to know they're up against a werewolf, vampire or shapeshifter. They might know how to fight that villain, but they still don't know who it is. The shapeshifter could be around them and so they need to be extra vigilant and that can add to the tension too.

However you choose to use your villain, or whether you let the reader in on the secret of who the villain is from the start, make certain you use the villain to get the most out of the conflict and that you can use that conflict to keep a fast pace in your story. Remember the villain is there to cause misery to your hero and/or heroine. The villain is the single person/entity who can keep the hero/heroine from getting what they want or prevent them from accomplishing their goals.

If you're not certain about how you're going to reveal your villain or if you want the person known from the start, try outlining or writing pages from the other angle. Instead of revealing the villain, don't do it. Then check to see if that works better for you. Does it heighten the tension? Does it make the pages go faster because the reader will want to find out the truth?

You can also try it the other way around. Instead of hiding the villain, make him known from the beginning and see how the story works in that case. This exercise might help you come up with new insight into your villain and your main characters, or it might help you discover new ways to conceal or use the villain.

All of these elements we've been discussing can determine exactly where and when you are going to expose the villain. You might even want to introduce the villain early to set up more powerful confrontations between the good guys and the villain. For instance, if you are writing a mystery series and the bad guy got away last time, knowing he or she is back in the picture can set up the latest installment on a whole new level and bring in further levels of tension. Waiting for him/her to return again in a later book can even make the situation or storyline more tense. Perhaps our hero and heroine have grown in knowledge and resources beyond where they were the last time they faced off with the villain. Now they might be more prepared to tackle him and his brand of evil so the reader wants to see a new struggle. That was certainly the case with Luke in *Star Wars*. He lost his hand in his face-to-face struggle with Darth Vader during *The Empire Strikes Back*. He also learned the startling truth of his parentage during that confrontation. When they face off again in *The Return of the Jedi*, he is a much more skilled fighter with his lightsaber, but he also is facing a personal struggle. We are ready to see them battle again, knowing he has grown. His father no longer has the element of surprise that he had the last time around, but now there are new issues. Is Luke going to be strong enough to defeat him, or could personal feelings get in the way? The fate of the Empire is at stake.

Think of the shark in the movie, *Jaws*. We knew Sheriff Brody, Hooper and Quint were facing a killer shark, which had already killed several people. It had attacked a boat and killed the entire crew. But we didn't know exactly how big it was until its full length was exposed alongside their boat. Can you blame Brody for his immediate reaction? "We're going to need a bigger boat."

We have come up with ideas for villains, motivations for good villains and looked at whether you are going to reveal them or keep them a secret until the end. Now, as we begin to wrap up, let's take a look at our villain's demise. In other words, how are you going to get "rid" of the villain?

Some of these ways to destroy the bad guys can be simple. Think of the use of water in *The Wizard of Oz*. No one realized the Wicked Witch could be destroyed that way. We knew she was vulnerable to a falling house. Consider the aliens in *War of The Worlds*. Who knew such powerful creatures could be wiped out by a tiny organism like a germ? The point is that you must establish their weaknesses as you create the villains – even if it is kept in your head until the end. You might give hints, but you must also be fair. For instance, in *The Wizard of Oz* we didn't ever see the Wicked Witch fly through a rainstorm and then have the aversion to water. The fact she could be destroyed by water was a total surprise. Also keep in mind that the creatures might evolve or change during your story, but there needs to be a force or reason behind it. The creatures in *Independence Day* were as susceptible to gunshots as a person, but the technology and shields in their spaceships protected them.

If your villain is a worthy villain, or equal in strength and cunning, or exceptionally smart and good at what he does, you might want your protagonist to finish him/her off in a way that is fitting to his personality. Thus, the space creatures in *Independence Day* were made vulnerable by a virus spreading from ship to ship, just like the satellites they used to cut off communications on Earth. The shark in Jaws chewed up everything so when he got a mouth full of pressurized air, Brody blew it up. Perhaps your hero is a cunning sharpshooter who places himself with the sun at his back so that it is in the face of the villain.

Will a simple bullet in the head work? Does there need to be, during the black moment and climax, a "fight" of some kind, whether physical or otherwise that will give the reader great satisfaction? Is there any better resolution than that dark, dark moment when all appears lost and suddenly the hero gets that last burst of strength that demolishes the giant or the stronger bad guy? Audiences and readers respond favorably to seeing their side win – especially when it comes from an unlikely source. The movie *Independence Day* had one of the most unlikely of heroes when the drunken ex-fighter pilot/crop duster who claimed he had once been kidnapped by aliens got to be the person who took out the alien spaceship and led the way for other pilots to demolish the rest of the force that was threatening the world.

Part of how you get rid of your villain depends on the genre of the story and on the degree of "badness" the villain has presented to the reader and the protagonist. It also depends on how the protagonist "feels" about the villain.

Perhaps the villain is not really such a bad person, but has only misinterpreted the facts. Once the hero/heroine sets him straight, the villain could change. That might be true in a romance where the villain-mother has been fighting the newlywed husband of the heroine. Once the older woman realizes she might lose her daughter, she could come to accept the new son-in-law.

The same might be true if you are dealing with a villain in a young adult novel, a time travel or a cozy mystery. The end result might not be death. The villain might go to jail or lose everything. He or she might simply be revealed so that the person can't continue to conduct whatever nefarious deeds they were doing to the hero or heroine. The villain might also change their ways – or at least promise to try.

For instance, in *Pride and Prejudice,* the villainous Wickham is not demolished. Instead, he is forced to marry Elizabeth's sister, Lydia. He gets a living, which he will probably squander, but he is stopped from trying to prey on rich young women and he now has a mother-in-law and flirtatious wife who will probably drive him crazy!

Let's look at some of the ways to finish off your villain:

> Direct battle where the main character kills him/her
>
> Another character kills him/her to save the main character
>
> He/she opts to commit suicide rather than be captured
>
> He/she is sent off into oblivion, another world or outer space
>
> He/she is left badly wounded so there is no longer a threat
>
> He/she is arrested and will go to jail
>
> He/she is turned over to enemies
>
> The villain loses the competition where he/she was cheating to win
>
> The hero/heroine rejects him/her and marries someone else

No matter what end you choose for your villain, he or she should know why or how the battle or competition was lost. If the villain lives, perhaps he/she has learned a lesson.

On the other hand, if you kill the villain, depending on how you kill him/her/it, you should be certain the villain knows/realizes who has killed him and why. If he has been doing all these bad things, he should know why, but maybe the hero or heroine can let him know how he was detected so that he knows he can no longer get away with his evil deeds. Even if he isn't going to jail this time, he has to stop his vile behavior or something horrible will happen to him next time around.

You should also be certain to give satisfaction to the hero or heroine or whoever does the deed of defeating the villain, but also you will want to give satisfaction to the reader in not only how the villain is uncovered, but how the hero or heroine has that final showdown with the villain and dispenses of him so that he is no longer a direct threat.

There are other ways to get rid of a villain too besides totally demolishing him or her. Perhaps the villain realizes the error of his/her ways and comes to his/her sense in the end.

For instance, Darth Vader is one of the most evil villains in outer space. Yet he comes full circle through the entire *Star Wars* saga, from Episode One where we see him as a young boy wanting to be a pilot, through manhood when he opts to become a villain and then as the quintessential bad guy through most of the second trilogy. But his son, Luke, sees something good in him. He thinks Darth Vader can be turned back from the Dark Side and in the final episode of the second trilogy, he accomplishes that goal. As Darth Vader dies, he turns away from the Dark Side to save his son. The villainous Empire is then defeated.

Be careful if you decide to do this.

You will need to show elements of that possibility before that final showdown if you chose to use this device. Again, you will want the readers to be satisfied and they won't be if it just happens without any previous indication that things might go this way.

If you are writing a series you may want to keep your villain around for future adventures. To do that you need to vanquish him during the book, but you don't necessarily want to destroy him. What you might choose to do is to let your villain escape before the end, as Vader did, so that the villain can return.

Again, if you do let the villain escape, be certain to give your readers a satisfying conclusion to that particular story. In *Star Wars – A New Hope,* Vader may have spun off into space, but Luke was able to destroy the Death Star and the rebels escaped capture. Now the rebels were free to move on with their next battle against the Empire in the next episode and the viewers were ready to see Vader again.

The same sort of ending came in the movie, *Alien*. That particular alien creature was destroyed but earlier in the movie we had seen there were dozens of eggs on the planet where the creature was found. It made sense that some of them might turn up again later and terrorize other crews, setting the stage for the next sequel when space colonists suddenly disappear and Ripley is forced to return to the planet with another space crew to find out what is happening to the settlers.

Hannibal Lecter was able to keep coming back as a villain because even though he was an evil killer, he was confined to prison. When author Thomas Harris introduced him in the first book, *Red Dragon*, detective Will Graham solved the case of who was killing families with Lecter's help, but the madman remained in prison.

When Lecter returned in the next book, *Silence of the Lambs*, he managed to escape. But the one thing he did at the end of that story was to let FBI heroine Claire Starling know that he wasn't coming after her even though he was free. Like Graham, Claire had solved her case of the worse villain, Buffalo Bill, but the man who helped her—Lecter—also got what he wanted—his freedom. In a twist to show that he wasn't going to necessarily change his ways, Lecter was shown setting out to seek revenge on the man who was HIS villain, the evil prison warden.

Author Thomas Harris was setting up the reader for any Hannibal story that might come up later. Readers knew he was still out there. *That* is another way to get rid of the bad villain – send him off to face an even worse villain.

The key here is what we mentioned earlier: if you don't kill off your bad guy or lock him up, you still have to provide a worthy, satisfactory ending to the current story. You can choose to let a villain live on or escape, but your plot will need a conclusion that will satisfy readers/viewers. They need to finish this book or movie knowing that whatever immediate threat was challenging the hero/heroine has ended.

Letting the Villain LIVE

In a sweet romance, you might have a villain, but more than likely your readers will not expect the villain to be killed. In one of these books, there probably won't be any violence at all and whatever the villain did may not be worthy of death. More likely it will be some sort of mental judgment or the future absence of something the villain cares about that will spell the doom or defeat for them.

In these cases, the ending depends on the degree of how bad the villain has been. In a sweet romance, the heroine might finally stand up to her evil father and let him know she is moving out and marrying the hero. The father's (villain) punishment is not death, but something that might be nearly as bad or worse. He has been secretly undermining the hero and keeping his daughter from the lad, but now the father realizes that not only has he lost his daughter to the man he hated, but he has probably lost her trust in *him*.

No longer is he the only man in her life, and he knows he won't be again. Even worse, she probably won't come to him for advice or trust him again, and it was all his own doing.

That heartbreak can be as devastating as death to a man used to having everything he wants and controlling everyone around him. Even worse he will have to see his daughter happier than she's ever been in her life, and he might be prevented from seeing the grandchildren she will probably have. If you are writing a sweet romance, you might choose to give him another chance and let him reconcile with his daughter.

In a cozy mystery, you might not kill the villain, but instead you might have the bad guy going to jail for a long term. That is what the readers want to see. They have spent their time trying to work out the clues to the puzzle and now they want to know that the bad guy gets the proper justice in the end.

They don't necessarily need the blood and guts violence or the shootout you might have in a thriller or suspense novel. They will be happy to see the bad guy or gal off the streets and to know that he/she will no longer be able to cause harm to anybody. They are not really bloodthirsty; they simply want him to get what's coming to him. In *Death on The Orient Express,* the dead man turned out to be so vile the killers were basically left to go their way.

As you work on your villains, keep in mind how you want them to come across to the reader/viewer. You want to create good strong villains so that they can be worthy adversaries for your hero and heroines.

The stronger your villains, the more resourceful and stronger your heroes and heroines must be to subdue them.

You want to give your readers a story that draws them in and that keeps them guessing throughout the book –until the ending – whether the hero and heroine will prevail. You want to end with a satisfying conclusion, even if the villain escapes justice. Under normal circumstances the ending should be that the hero/heroine defeats the villain, but it might also be that the villain escapes this time around.

If you choose to go in that direction, where the villain escapes, be certain to give the reader a satisfying conclusion to this story. The hero/heroine should get some satisfaction in a different way. Perhaps the villain escapes capture, but the hero and heroine have found each other, or perhaps, like Wickham, the villain has gone on to a torturous future.

The main point is not to let your readers down when you are finishing off the villain or sending him/her away at the end. Give the reader a good ending by providing a realistic and justified finish for your bad guy so the reader will want to keep coming back for more of your books or stories.

A twist at the end is not necessarily a bad thing.

What you want your villain to do is to give the reader a good story and if it means they get away to battle your hero another day, well, the choice is yours to make as the author. You can do whatever you think will be best for the hero, the villain, and future stories.

In the movie, *Pulp Fiction,* several of the bad guys get away at the end of the movie, but with different results. The lovers who started out to rob everyone in the café get a lesson that they may be bad, but there are even worse villains around them, and they might want to think twice next time they set out to commit a robbery. The boxer and his girlfriend get away, but he has faced almost certain death and he has lost his "LA privileges." He can't afford to come back to town. We already know that Vincent has little time to live once he leaves the cafe while Jules has decided to give up his evil life and simply wants to wander the world.

Villains Who Come to a Great Ending

Aliens – *War of the Worlds*
The Shark – *Jaws*
King Kong – *King Kong*
Jules Winnfield – *Pulp Fiction*

CHAPTER 9

Minor and Misc. Villains

*Give me the good old days of heroes and villains,
the kind you can bravo or hiss.*
Bette Davis

While villains can vary from light-hearted bad guys to bullying classmates, from nasty jealous rivals to vicious serial killers to evil creatures in outer space, your main villain should stand out in the story. We have mentioned that several times. That doesn't mean you can't have plenty of other minor villains around causing problems for your characters and giving trouble to your hero and heroine or even to the main villain himself. This person or thing doesn't necessarily have to be a sidekick to the villain. On the contrary, you can easily have other, lesser villains present in any story. They might even be suspected of being the main villain in a murder mystery. Villains who are actually the *red herring* may take as much care to create as the main villain, since all the clues may need to point in their direction. Let's examine some of these *other* villains:

> In a **light romance,** the lesser villain might be the ex-girlfriend of the hero or the soon-to-be mother-in-law who is simply causing mischief without meaning

to while the main villain is trying to break apart the couple.

In a **thriller**, there may be a lesser villain cooking up his or her own plot that gets overshadowed by the main villain's deeds.

In a **murder mystery** it might be the friend of the murder victim who happened to be in the wrong place at the wrong time and now he is trying to hide his presence at the scene.

Remember, not all villains are totally evil. Let's review some of the different kinds and different levels of opposing forces.

Antagonists

The Antagonist may not be the main villain in the story but can cause lots of problems just the same. We mentioned this type of character earlier. The Antagonist is a character who works in "opposition" to the hero or heroine by simply trying to prevent them from achieving their goals, but this person might not be the cause of the direct problem in the story.

While villains can be Antagonists, not all Antagonists are villains. Take Samuel Gerard from *The Fugitive*, for instance. Gerard is an antagonist as he is in opposition to Richard Kimble's (our hero) escape and tries to re-capture him. He is not a villain. He has no evil intentions to others at large. He is simply trying to thwart the hero by capturing him and taking him back to jail. The real villain is the one-armed man who killed Kimble's wife.

You might consider Golem in the *Lord of the Rings* books as an Antagonist. He was up to no good, but he was not one of the main villains that Frodo faced, such as Sauron. He was simply a sad creature who had been bewitched by the Ring and wanted it more than anything.

Then there are those people who start out as possible villains and then either switch sides or aren't as bad as they seem. For instance, Lando Calrissian in *The Empire Strikes Back* started out as a friend to Han. Then he turned on him, but he had a reason – he was trying to help his people at the colony where he was in control. His motive for helping the bad guys was to protect his people. Unfortunately, they chose to let the bounty hunters take Han. Eventually, Lando sided with the rebel forces in their battle against the Empire.

Creatures/Aliens

Otherworldly creatures who act as villains have long been popular in movies and books. We all have probably watched at least one zombie movie or read a vampire book and we have seen aliens come in all shapes and sizes from planets or unknown destinations all over the universe. Tolkien brought them to us from Middle Earth.

In the cases of these creature-villains, you might have a particular leader or person/creature who is the embodiment of evil leading the others. If you have the urge to write such a story, go for it. Make believe creatures can come from anywhere. Only your imagination will hold you back. They can be anything from snakes on the loose, to giant spiders to dinosaurs to evolving aliens to sharks coming out of tornadoes.

How do you make your story work for the maximum effect? Let's look at some of those creatures and entities and how to create them for maximum effect:

The creatures should start out as infallible. This means they can't be stopped when they began their reign of terror. If they can be destroyed easily, the story is over. They have to seem like they are so strong that nothing can stop them, even if it just means that a serum hasn't been discovered that can defeat them. Think of the many diseases that seemed like they couldn't be stopped but after years of research they were eventually defeated. Think of your villain-creatures that way but on a much-accelerated timeline.

If a creature or disease can be conquered or is fallible, then your story will need to go in another direction. That means either a villain is protecting the creature or hiding the truth about the disease or monster. A good example of that are the dinosaurs of *Jurassic Park*. They're fine as long as they are kept on islands near South America, but turn one loose in San Diego and people are going to die. Putting them into an enclosed environment is not the answer either – not when a company is weighing protecting the public or saving the animals. Saving a virus was the premise in *Outbreak*, where a general was ready to demolish a town to protect the secret of a virus the government wanted for future use against enemies.

The creatures can come in hoards or be solitary. Think of a virus that takes over the city or spreads. It might be claiming lots of victims, but it is just one entity and finding the cure for the virus or discovering the serum that will destroy it, will also put an end to the mayhem. That was the premise in the original *War of the Worlds*. Updating that idea, it was a computer virus that proved to be the key in the *Independence Day* series. In both cases, the hordes of enemies from outer space appeared invincible at first. But one small bug – and later a computer bug – proved to be stronger.

The creatures, aliens or virus should be strong and deadly.

Getting a cold might make you uncomfortable, but you know if you stay in bed for a while you'll get better. But what happens if people around you start getting a disease that kills them in a couple of days?

Now you need to worry about either catching it yourself or losing others to it. The stakes are higher, especially if you don't know how the disease is transmitted or how to combat it. The same is true if you are writing of a creature or an alien entity. If you are looking for traits or strengths to give to otherworldly creatures, consider reading some of the Greek, Roman or Norse myths for gods or creatures that were infallible.

The story itself must be told on a personal level. There needs to be a personal side to the overall tale. No matter how big an attack or how widespread the virus is, readers are going to react better if you tell the story from a personal level. Readers want to know about *someone* who is threatened by the virus or creature, not simply a large group of people.

The entire earth may be in danger, but if you tell the story of how *one* town or one family copes with the onslaught, then readers, movie and TV viewers are going to be more responsive. Whether it is one family fighting off aliens, like in *Signs* or the new *War of the Worlds,* or a whole town facing disaster, as the families and doctors in *Outbreak*, it is the individual people who are experiencing the attacks and who may face extinction that make us care what happens.

Include likable characters/creatures. This may sound strange because if you are writing a science fiction or fantasy story, the story may not include human characters. They might all be from other planets or other worlds. But the main characters in your story who are threatened personally need to be at least a little likable.

Will we want to see the hero succeed if he is a jerk? Would we want that in any story? No. And we don't want to see that in a science fiction or fantasy either.

We want our heroes and heroines to be someone or something we can root for. While Mr. Spock never showed emotion, he was curious and confused by it and that drew viewers to him. The space creature in The *Shape of Water* was strangely vulnerable, as were the creatures in *Avatar*.

The creature needs a weakness. Whether it is a climate that is unfavorable to them or whether it is the discovery of the magic potion that will stop the creatures or virus, there needs to be a way to achieve some sort of victory for our heroes and heroines. This means you need to study your creature/villain and figure out the details of who or what it is. The good part about this is that YOU are in charge. You can give the villain any sort of weakness you want. It is totally your choice. But once you have made that decision you need to be fair with it.

There should be a resolution. It might be that the space creatures pack up and leave, like they did in *Signs* when they discovered the earth wasn't a good place for them. It might be that the predatory animals are left on an island with only warnings to keep others away (as in the *Jurassic Park* franchise) but the story itself needs to have some sort of conclusion.

Your story location can be a villain. From the hotel in *The Shining* to the desert town of *Desperation*, Nevada, Stephen King has often made settings the very essence of the villain in a story. Both were hard to get to, but the hotel in *The Shining* was inaccessible in the winter. It meant that the ghosts that wandered it were free to work whatever kind of chaos they wanted at the Overlook Hotel. The fact that it was so isolated meant the good guys (Danny and Wendy) were on their own.

Don't be afraid to improvise. This is your story and the only limits are your own imagination. Dream up your own world, make up your own overall rules and then let your characters and creatures follow them. Once you have those rules established, as long as you and your characters follow them or logically break them, you can do whatever you choose to do. Your characters and your creatures—good and bad—are at your mercy, as are your heroes and heroines.

As you create new worlds and creatures, you can make them as strong or peaceful as you want. If you are writing a story with otherworldly villains, the plot could revolve around life or death situations, but it doesn't need to.

You might turn things around so it is a love story where the hero and heroine are aliens or one is.

You get to choose.

As we have mentioned, villains don't need to be the foreign or space creatures. The villains can be selfish earthlings trying to destroy the alien. Since you are telling the story you have the ability to determine who or what is good and who the villain is. Use those powers to tell a great story!

Great Minor/Other Villains

Golem – *Lord of the Rings*
Jabba the Hutt – *Star Wars*
The Iceberg -- *Titanic*

CHAPTER 10

Summary

The villain allows you to let loose of your creativity.
Jodi Piccoult

Now that we have put our villains together and put them into the story in starring or secondary roles, let's take a final look at how to use the villain. Then we will finish with a checklist on how to tell if your villains are ready for the story.

Let's begin with a review of a few things to keep in mind as you craft your villains:

Villains should be guided by the genre and tone of the story.

We've said this before, but it's worth repeating as we wrap up. A villain in a cozy mystery or a sweet romance will be very different from the hard-edged, nasty villain in a thriller, suspense, science fiction or fantasy book. For instance, in a thriller or fantasy, the villain might be so totally evil that their entire purpose in life is to take over the world, or to destroy everything and everyone around them. Murder and killing come easy to this villain.

There may be no redeeming this character. He/she will always be evil. Given other circumstances this villain will always want to have the last say and be in charge of the world. The Emperor in the *Star Wars* saga and Sauron in *Lord of the Rings* wanted total control. They were willing to go to any lengths to subjugate planets and races. The villains that superheroes like Superman or Spiderman faced are often the same type – from Lex Luthor to The Joker, they don't care who or how many people get hurt.

On the other hand, if you are writing a mystery or suspense novel, the villain might be mean and nasty but he might also not be quite as bad. Consider the difference between the two villains in *Romancing the Stone*. Ralph was a bumbling antagonist, but Colonel Zolo was a cold-hearted killer. One led an army that could easily kill, while the other was constantly in danger of being killed by his own bungling.

Create villains readers can love to hate.

When you consider the villain, normally the person would be someone who is evil, crass, dishonest or who has traits that make the person easily disliked. But this is not always true. At times writers will create redeemable villains or other characters who go from being the bad guy to showing they were carrying out their vile actions for good or personal reasons, and perhaps now they have seen the error of their ways.

Let's go back to Darth Vader. Through the original *Star Wars* episodes, we didn't know why he had become so evil. He did save his son at the end, so we knew there had to be some humanity left inside that dark shell. What made him turn to the Dark Side? In the first three episodes, we finally get his story from young pilot to Jedi knight. In that trilogy we discover how his beloved mother was tortured and killed, how he fell in love with Luke and Leia's mother and why he eventually lost faith in the Jedis. While this part of the series is often criticized, we still get a picture of what transformed him from a young, impressionable boy into the totally evil creature we were introduced to in the very first *Star Wars* movie in 1977. To this day, Darth Vader remains one of the best-known villains of all time.

There are many other types of villains who can grab the reader and hold their attention, which is why writers continue to develop them and use them in their stories of all genres. In many cases, the readers don't know if they are rooting for or against them. Another complex villain/hero is Heathcliff in the romance *Wuthering Heights*. Here is a man so consumed with love and hate he is willing to make everyone around him miserable because of the loss he suffered. He is the villain and yet he will always be the doomed Cathy's tragic romantic hero.

Bring the villain into your story early

While you can bring a villain in at any point in your book and show who they are, their deeds should be visible almost from the beginning and should continue to cause problems. You can always make something that the villain does part of your Inciting Incident or his/her actions can be what sets the plot in motion. In a mystery or thriller, the villain usually sets up the events that get the plot moving with either a murder or attack. In a romance the villain can begin to cause problems for the hero and the heroine before they even meet.

Give your villain a goal and make it personal

Just like your hero and heroine, your villain should have a goal from the very beginning of the book. Even if you don't show it immediately, you should have it in your head. That is why you need to create your villain and know exactly where your villain is at all times.

You will not be able to make them react unless they have a reason. Even if evil aliens in Alien had a reason for what the creature was doing. He wanted to live and it was important it get off the dead planet. To do that it was trying to get on the space ship using a human host. And it would have stayed on that space ship until it took it to another planet where it could once again feed.

Just as your hero and heroine's goal might change as the story progresses, the villain's goal might change too, and that is why it should be personal. The villain should have as much of a personal interest in the outcome of the story as the hero or heroine. Make them care enough to want to do evil things.

Don't let your villain disappear

The villain needs to be visible throughout the story. It might be tempting, especially in a romance to have him/her do one or two bad things in the beginning and then lose sight of him as you develop the love story or as you try to solve the mystery. Make certain your villain continues to play some sort of role throughout the book. As we've said before an evil deed or manipulation by the bad guy can help to create conflict and increase the tension.

Some villains are redeemable.

If you are writing a sweet romance or inspirational book, the villain will be much tamer than the bad guy in a thriller. The antagonist might be the mother of the hero or the neighbor next door. The motive might be a desire to keep the couple apart or to steal the family ranch. It may be someone who simply tries to come between the couple in a romance.

In a cozy mystery, the villain might be the mayor of a town who accidentally kills the banker who was threatening to expose him.

Normally he might not kill anyone, but unusual circumstances have led him to extreme actions in this case.

These are people who aren't psychopaths or necessarily mentally disturbed. Other forces led these villains into their bad behavior. The mayor might be going to jail, but he probably wouldn't kill again.

The mother-in-law in the romance may even see the error of her ways and stop being a villain because she has decided she doesn't want to lose the opportunity of spending time with her grandchildren. Some villains are redeemable while others must be destroyed. As the author, you get to make the choice.

It is difficult to say which villains might turn out to be redeemable. Consider the case of Darth Vader who tried for years to bring his son over to the dark side of the Force. He has done everything in his power to win him over to his side, including revealing his paternity and then bringing Luke to the Emperor. In the end, though, his love for his son leads him to sacrifice himself to save Luke.

In most cases, the evil villain may still have to die for all the terrible things he/she has done. In other, milder cases, the villain might be allowed to live and might even be given another chance. But that requires special circumstances and the story itself must still be wrapped up with the hero and heroine getting some sort of resolution that is believable.

Don't lose sight of your story arc.

As you write your stories, one thing to remember as you direct your plot is that the hero/heroine's arcs are in direct opposition to that of the villain. As we discussed in a previous chapter, when the villain's arc is up, the arc for the hero and heroine are down. Since the story ends with the hero or heroine being successful in vanquishing the villain at the end, the villain's arc should be at the bottom or low.

The villain's arc will be at its highest just before the climax. At this point the villain should be on the verge of success. The hero or heroine may think he/she is licked but the character is ready to give it one last struggle. The villain feels like he/she has won and is ready to claim victory. Then comes the massive climax where the good guys win out.

Even if the bad guys do somehow manage to get away, they should be on the run and not celebrating any sort of victory. In order to see how this works, try constructing the villain's arc alongside the main character's arc.

Some mystery writers say that they write the villain's story totally separately to see what they are doing every day, even if that part of the story never makes it into the book. Knowing how the killer reacts or what the killer is planning next or what the bad guy is thinking can help the writer to see more clearly the role of the villain.

Give the reader a satisfying end to the villain

Normally, in most books, movies and plays, the villain is going to be discovered and vanquished. He or she is going to jail, going to die, going to repent or be destroyed. If you are dealing with a whole army of villains, the hero's men and/or women are going to come out on top.

The opposing force will be defeated. But sometimes, particularly if you are writing a series, the bad guy may get away. If that happens, the hero or heroine should have still accomplished something. Perhaps they have solved the current crime and they know who the villain is now so that next time they will be more prepared to do battle.

Letting the villain get away doesn't let them off the hook, and you still need to bring the current story to a satisfying conclusion. There needs to be some sort of resolution, even if it is learning the need to be more vigilant the next time.

You can have more than one villain.

Yes, some books have more than one villain. Let's look at a couple of very different genres, historical romantic fiction and thriller.

In Jane Austen's, *Pride and Prejudice,* one of the most peaceful romantic stories you might find, there are actually several villains. First, we have Mr. Bingley's sisters who conspire to keep him from Jane and belittle her to him all the time.

Next, we have Mr. Wickham who is up to no good with his constant lies. He is charming to Elizabeth, but he has no problem changing his affections to Lydia. Then he runs off with her. He probably wouldn't have married her, if Mr. Darcy hadn't intervened. We also have Lady Catherine trying to marry Darcy to her daughter.

In *Silence of the Lambs*, we have the main killer, Buffalo Bill who is killing young women and skinning them. Clarice Starling must help to track him down. But to do that she must talk to Hannibal Lecter, a man who is utterly evil himself. He might not be killing people now, but we know he has done it in the past and when he starts getting inside her head, she begins to discover just how bad he really is.

We have reached the end, but the future is ahead for you and your villains. As we wrap up, we leave you with a list for developing your own villains.

Please use it to create your own villain checklist that you can use to plot your next book. Who knows, you could end up developing the next great, memorable villain.

Villain Checklist

Does the villain's first deed show up early?

Does your villain have an important enough role?

How bad will your villain be?

What is his/her biggest strength?

What is his/her major weakness?

What is his/her overall goal?

What will be an early success for the villain?

What is the villain doing to create friction between main characters?

What is an early setback for the villain?

What does the villain do in retaliation?

What are some small problems (troubles) the villain can cause?

How will he/she be destroyed?

Will this villain return in a future book?

Start constructing your villains as you build your heroes and heroines. Knowing them as well as you do your heroes/heroines can help to develop your plot.

Understanding motives help you figure out how they might accomplish their goals and why they want to run roughshod over the hero and/or heroine. Knowing their relationship to the hero before you tell the reader allows you and the villain to work behind the scenes to manipulate the plot and your main characters.

Don't be afraid to experiment with *all* your characters, especially the villains. They can be every bit as important as the main characters. The choices are yours and who knows, you may create the next round of villains that readers will never forget.

Villains Gallery
From A through Z

If you're undecided or uncertain about your villains, here is an overall list of some of our favorite bad characters and evildoers of all designs and nasty dispositions. They come from books, movies, television and plays. Some we've already mentioned, but this overall list might give your ideas as you fashion your own bad guys. They come in all shapes, sizes, sexes and some are out of this world or from the inner world!

A   Aliens – *War of the Worlds, Independence Day*
          Anthony, Bruno – *Strangers on a Train*
          Audrey II – *Little Shop of Horrors*
          Captain Ahab – *Moby Dick*

B   Norman Bates – *Psycho*
          Patrick Bateman – *American Psycho*

Ernst Biofeld – *Thunderball*
Captain Bligh – *Mutiny on the Bounty*
The Bride – *Kill Bill*

C   Tony Camonte – *Scarface*
Max Cady – *Cape Fear*
Catwoman – *Batman*
Jimmy Conway -- *Goodfellas*
Michael Corleone – *The Godfather Trilogy*
Noah Cross – *Chinatown*

D   Mrs. Danvers, *Rebecca*
Cruella de Ville – *101 Dalmations*
Count Dracula - *Dracula*

E   Bob Ewell – *To Kill a Mockingbird*
Dr. Evil – *Austin Powers*

F   Jezzie Flannigan – *Along Came a Spider*
Alex Forrest – *Fatal Attraction*
Frankenstein – *Bride of Frankenstein*

G   Gordon Gekko -- *Wall Street*
Auric Goldfinger – *Goldfinger*
Felonious Gru – *Despicable Me*

Hans Gruber – *Die Hard*

H	Hal 9000 – *2001, A Space Odyssey*
Henry Hill -- *Goodfellas*
Captain Hook - *Peter Pan*
Gillian Holroyd – *Bell, Book and Candle*
Ian Howe – *National Treasure*

I	Iago - *Othello*

J	The Jackal – *Day of the Jackal*
Inspector Javert – *Les Miserables*
The Joker – *Batman*

K	Kahn – *Star Trek*
Ivan Korshunov – *Air Force One*
Freddy Krueger – *A Nightmare on Elm Street*

L	Johnny Lawrence – *The Karate Kid*
Hannibal Lecter -- The *Silence of the Lambs*
Loki – *Thor*
Lex Luther -- *Superman*

M	Magneto – *The X-Men*
Medusa – *The Clash of the Titans*
Fernand Mondego – *Count of Monte Cristo*

Professor Moriarty – *Sherlock Holmes*

N   Nikita -- *Le Femme Nikita*

O   Danny Ocean – *Ocean's Eleven*

P   Poison Ivy, *Batman*
         Mr. Potter – *It's a Wonderful Life*
         Miranda Priestly – *The Devil Wears Prada*

Q   The Evil Queen – *Snow White*
         Captain Hank Quinlin – *Touch of Evil*

R   Nurse Ratched – *Cuckoo's Nest*
         Principal Rooney – *Ferris Bueller's Day Off*

S   Saruman – *Lord of the Rings*
         Satan – The *Bible*
         Stepmother -- *Cinderella*
         William Stranix – *Under Siege*

T   The Terminator – *The Terminator*
         Jack Torrance – *The Shining*
         Catherine Trammell – *Basic Instinct*

U   Ultron – *Avenger* Series
         Frank Underwood – *House of Cards*

V   Darth Vader – *Star Wars*
          Vincent Vega – *Pulp Fiction*
          Lord Voldemort – *Harry Potter* Series
          Jason Voorhees – *Friday the 13th*

W   Marsellus Wallus – *Pulp Fiction*
          Annie Wilkes -- *Misery*
          The Wicked Witch -- *The Wizard of Oz*

XYZ   General Zod – *Man of Steel*
          Zombies – *Dawn of the Dead*

BEFORE YOU GO...

Thank you for reading **Creating Great Villains**. We hope you enjoyed it and are ready to start your own writing project! This is the fourth book in the Let's Write a Story series. The first three are:

      Seven Ways to Plot

      Creating Memorable Characters

      The Plotting Wheel

The next books *Let's Write a Story* series are:

-       **Creating Unforgettable Flaws**

- *Character Driven Plotting*
- *Creating your Character's ARC*

AUTHORS

Sue Viders

Sue has a BFA in education and fine arts and is the author of 25 non-fiction books. She has written extensively for a variety of magazines and newspapers. A national columnist for years on art marketing in *The Artist's Magazine*, Sue has spoken to various organizations nationally and internationally on marketing and writing for over thirty-five years. She regularly teaches online

Her other books for writers include *The Complete Writer's Guide to HEROES and HEROINES, Sixteen Master Archetypes,* and the *PICK a NUMBER* series.

Meg and the Mysterious Voices, is the first in a series of light-hearted cozy mysteries revolving around Meg Jamison, a middle-aged artist with an interesting hearing aid, a pair of silver earrings, that allows Meg to not only hear better but to hear a person's inner thoughts.

Becky Martinez

Becky Martinez is a former broadcast journalist who worked in TV newsrooms for 30 years and 5 years in public relations before turning to writing full time. She is published in nonfiction, mystery, romance, and romantic suspense. She also teaches writing classes online and has presented workshops and panels at national/regional writing conferences, such as Romance Writers of America, RomCon, Colorado Gold, Emerald Cities Writers Conference and Left Coast Crime.

She writes fiction as Rebecca Grace. Her novella, *Shadows from the Past,* was released in 2019 on audio. Her previous mystery & suspense novels include *Blues at 11, Dead Man's Rules* and *Deadly Messages.* She has a weekly blog http://www.rebecca-grace.blogspot.com and her latest classes and works are listed on her website at http://www.rebeccagrace.com

Together Sue and Becky have the following website:

Writethatnovel.net

Email us at:

sueviders@comcast.net

beckmartinez77@aol.com

NONFICTION BOOKS for Writers

The Complete Writer's Guide to Heroes and Heroines, Sixteen Master Archetypes by Sue Viders

www.amazon.com

The book's guidelines provide insight into how archetypes are formed and how they interact with other archetypes.

Writing a Novel, A Step by Step WORKBOOK and GUIDE by Sue Viders

www.amazon.com

Ever wanted to write a novel but didn't know where to start and wanted a bit of guidance. Lots of helpful comments to assist you with your story and plenty of room to physically write out your ideas before starting on the computer.

PICK a NUMBER series - by Sue Viders

www.amazon.com

Writing books for the aspiring author based on the movies and TV. Each of the ten books in the series is 6x9 with lots of movie and TV examples — over 500 in each book — plus room for the writer to make notes as how some of these ideas and suggestions might be helpful in their story.

Book 1 - *START a STORY - OVERVIEW*
Book 2 - *CHOOSE a GENRE*

Book 3 - *DEVELOP a CHARACTER*
Book 4 - *FIND a PLOT*
Book 5 - *SELECT a SETTING*
Book 6 - *DEVELOP GOALS and MOTIVATION*
Book 7 - *SECONDARY CHARACTERS*
Book 8 - *CREATE a CONFLICT*
Book 9 - *CHOOSE a THEME*
Book 10 - *ENDINGS*

FICTION BOOKS

Sue Viders
- The Meg Jamison Mysteries - www.amazon.com

- Book 1 - *Meg and the Mysterious Voices*

- Book 2 - *Meg and the Misguided Arsonist*

Becky Martinez
Available at www.bn.com, www.amazon.com or www.thewildrosepress.com
- *Blues at 11*

- *Dead Man's Rules*
- *Shadows from the Past* (now on Audio)
- *The Problem*
- *Deadly Messages*
- *Home Fires Burning* – Wings ePress
- *Love on Deck* – Wings ePress

One More Romance -- Heart of Denver Romance Writers Anthology

www.ingramcontent.com/pod-product-compliance
Lightning Source LLC
Chambersburg PA
CBHW051652040426
42446CB00009B/1105